William J. Gentsch

Gentsch's Dictionary of Detroit and Its Vicinity

William J. Gentsch

Gentsch's Dictionary of Detroit and Its Vicinity

ISBN/EAN: 9783337861711

Printed in Europe, USA, Canada, Australia, Japan

Cover: Foto ©Thomas Meinert / pixelio.de

More available books at **www.hansebooks.com**

S. DOW ELWOOD,   D. M. FERRY,   WM. STAGG,   WM. A. MOORE,
    President.   Vice-President.   Ass't Sec'y and Treas.   Attorney.

DIRECTORS:

THOMAS W. PALMER,	E. H. FINN,	WM. A. MOORE,
H. KIRKE WHITE,	FRANCIS ADAMS,	JEROME CROUL,
D. M. FERRY,	WM. S. GREEN,	S. DOW ELWOOD.

Wayne County Savings Bank,

DETROIT.

4 Per Cent. Interest Allowed on Deposits.

N. B —Exclusively a Bank for Savings and Trust Funds.

To the Board of Directors of the Wayne County Savings Bank:

    I herewith submit the Forty-Second Semi-Annual Statement of the condition of this Bank, at the close of business January 7, 1893.   Very respectfully,

                                              S. DOW ELWOOD, President.

RESOURCES.

Loans—On Collaterals,	$1,522,043.77
" On Real Estate,	1,025,914.89
" Invested in Municipal Bonds,	2,546,383.18
	$5,094,341.84
Real Estate—Banking House and Lot,	110,000.00
Other Real Estate,	40,148.62
Cash on hand,	1,095,783.89
Total,	$6,340,274.35

LIABILITIES.

Capital Stock paid in,	$ 150,000.00
Surplus Fund,	150,000.00
Reserve Fund,	150,000.00
	$ 450,000.00
Undivided Profits,	148,874.8
Savings Deposits,	5,741,399.
Total,	$6,340,274.
INTEREST.	
Due and accrued on Loans and Investments,	$75,00

HAVE YOU SEEN

That Map of the city showing the . relative . position . of . your store to the railways?

DO YOU KNOW

That your Out of Town Customers can find you easily by consulting our Map?

DO YOU KNOW

That it will be handy alike for the Buyer as well as for the Seller?

TZEN & GENTSCH,
PUBLISHERS.

The Largest and Most Complete Printing Establishment in the State of Michigan.

John Bornman & Son,

Successors to

O. S. Gulley, Bornman & Co.,

FINE BOOK AND JOB

PRINTERS,

 12, 14, 16 & 18 East Larned Street,
DETROIT.

Illustrated Catalogue and Fine Commercial Printing of Every Description a Specialty.

DETROIT'S GREAT HEALTH RESORT.

Clark's Riverside Mineral Springs
BATH HOUSE,

FORT STREET WEST, CORNER CLARK AVE.

Ladies' Department open Daily from 7.00 A. M. to 8.00 P. M.   Gents' Department open Daily from 7.00 A. M. to 8.00 P. M.   Take Fort Street Cars direct to the Springs. Open Daily from 7.00 A. M. to 8.00 P. M.   Accommodations for Ladies and Gentlemen.

DISEASES SUCCESSFULLY TREATED:

Rheumatism, Chronic, Inflammatory, Sciatica, Muscular. Skin Diseases, Eczema, Salt Rheum, Scrofula. Blood Poisoning from any cause whatever.
Female Diseases, Neuralgia, Dyspepsia, Catarrh, Kidney and Bladder Troubles.

A. S. CLARK, Proprietor, DETROIT, Mich.

GENTSCH'S
DICTIONARY OF DETROIT

AND ITS VICINITY

WITH MAPS AND ILLUSTRATIONS.

Containing Full Information Regarding Industries, Societies, Amusements, Resorts, Etc., in and near Detroit, Arranged Alphabetically.

W. J. GENTSCH, PUBLISHER,
12 TO 18 LARNED STREET EAST,

1893

Entered according to Act of Congress, in the year 1892, by

W. J. GENTSCH,

In the office of the Librarian of Congress, at Washington, D. C.

———

All rights reserved.

PREFACE.

This being the first edition, it will not be quite as perfect as it is hoped to make succeeding issues, but no time or expense has been spared in gathering all valuable information. It is arranged alphabetically; therefore no index is necessary. Any information regarding a particular place will be found under its proper heading, with description and correct location; for instance, the art schools will be found by turning to the A's, chamber of commerce under the C's, parks under the P's, etc. This work is not an advertising scheme. Wherever advertisements are inserted they appear as such, and not in disguise. It fills a legitimate field, comprising important information in one book, that has heretofore only been given in sections and at random, and much of which, though valuable, has never been published before.

The information contained in this dictionary has been obtained whenever possible, from official quarters, and is therefore authentic and reliable.

WILLIAM T. DUST,

BUILDERS' AND GENERAL

HARDWARE.

Repairs for All Stoves.

STATE AGENT FOR LEHIGH FURNACES.

TIN, COPPER AND SHEET IRON WORK.

House Furnishings, Stoves, Ranges, Oils, Glass, Mechanics' Tools.

566 and 568 MONROE AVE.
200 to 212 ST. AUBIN AVE.

'PHONE 1788-3 R.

DETROIT, MICH.

GENTSCH'S
DICTIONARY OF DETROIT

AND ITS VICINITY.

Abandoned or Lost Property, when found by Detroit police, is turned over to police headquarters, cor. of Bates and Randolph streets. Articles left on the horse cars, electric roads or ferry boats, may be recovered by applying at the respective offices of these companies.

Abattoirs.—The largest abattoir in Detroit is located on Dix ave. and Michigan Central R. R. It is the property of the Michigan Beef and Provision Co.; office is located on Cadillac Square. There are several smaller abattoirs, but they are used only for retail trade.

African Methodist Episcopal Churches.—The following list gives the names and location of those in Detroit:

Bethel A. M. E. Church, corner Napoleon and Hastings streets.

Brown's A. M. E. Church, corner Thirtieth and Jackson streets.

Ebenezer A. M. E. Church, north side Calhoun, bet. Beaubien and St. Antoine streets.

Aldermen.—The legislative power of the city is vested in a common council, composed of 32 members, who must be qualified electors, one of whom is elected in each ward of the city, at the annual city election, for the term of two years, from the second Tuesday of January next ensuing their election. They have power to enforce, pass, and repeal city ordinances, subject to the approval of the mayor, and to pass resolutions over his veto by a three-quarters vote. They meet at their own pleasure, usually once a week, but occasionally at greater intervals, in their room in the City Hall.

Ambulances.—An ambulance service is connected with the Harper, Grace and Emergency hospitals, and also at 283 Rivard street, under the charge of the City Poor Commission. Boyd's ambulance, located at the same place, is engaged by railroad companies and a few larger corporations. All the patrol wagons in the police service are so equipped that they may be instantly used as an ambulance. (See Horse Ambulance.)

Amusements.—Detroit is well provided with amusements, both summer and winter; in the latter the three large opera houses and

Wonderland Musee are always in full blast, and this year the Lyceum has inaugurated a season of summer opera. Wonderland Musee will be open nearly if not quite all summer, and there will be summer opera at Des-Chree-Shos-Ka, an island resort, eight miles down the river, besides the usual skating and other pastimes in winter, boating, excursions, and many other amusements in summer.

Architectural Features.—Detroit has many fine buildings, both public and private, of modern construction. Among those erected in the last few years are the Hammond, an office building, ten stories high, exterior of brown stone and brick, interior mainly of iron, and finished from top to bottom with white marble. It is perfectly fire proof. The Hudson building is of a different type, being for retail business; it is also built of brown stone and brick, eight stories high, and one of the many attractions to be found in it is an observing tower on the top, from which a splendid view can be obtained. The two Union depots are fine examples of modern building; other fine buildings are the Campau, Newberry and McMillan, Moffatt, Whitney, Hodges, McGraw, Board of Trade, Cadillac Hotel, Russell House, Ste. Claire Hotel, Court House, City Hall, Public Library, Art Museum, Detroit Opera House, Lyceum Theatre, Whitney's Opera House, and many others too numerous to mention, ranging in height from five to ten stories. A trip up Woodward avenue or out Jefferson avenue, by electric car or by carriage, both streets being paved with asphalt, would show many fine churches and private dwellings, built of brown stone, white stone, white marble, various colored brick, and many other odd but pleasing materials; mention should also be made of the new post office, which is in course of construction, of white stone, occupying an entire block, and which will be the finest and largest building in this part of the country; the new Chamber of Commerce building, now being built, will also be a very fine building.

Art Museum.—This building is located on Jefferson avenue and Hastings street, and is an imposing and beautiful edifice, situated as it is in the midst of elegant private residences. The Museum contains hundreds of fine paintings, statues, interesting relics, curiosities, etc., constantly being added to; it also has a large class of art students, which is growing in size every year.

Art Schools.—No city in the country offers better facilities for the cultivation of the fine arts. It has long been known as a musical centre, and during the past few years has made rapid progress in the study of art. This interest is largely due to the refined taste of the people, whose wealth enables them to gratify a love of the beautiful, the esult being several private collections of great value. There is are important school connected with the Art Museum (for location, see Art Museum), with 200 students in attendance during the past year. There is a fine corps of teachers; one of the largest collections of casts in the west, while the museum and gallery offer the greatest advantage for the study of art in the country. Several teachers of ability give private lessons in their studios, and the vast field of varied scenery, within easy access of the city, make summer classes in out-door sketching both popular and profitable.

THE DETROIT SCHOOL OF ARTS is located corner Grand River and Washington avenues. The school is open daily from September 1st to June 17. The object of this school is to afford facilities for study of the highest order to all those seeking education in the various branches of art. Its most important mission, perhaps, is to place within reach of the artisan, as well as the person of wealth and leisure, the opportunity of increasing his artistic knowledge and skill in the direct lines in which lie his life work. In the industrial or applied arts there is the greatest need for more artistic skill on the part of the workman and designer, and it is proposed to make the work of this institution of practical value to decorators, designers, woodcarvers, lithographers, engravers, photographers, metal workers, silversmiths, etc., as well as to those who wish to follow the higher branches, and make a profession of painting or sculpture; or those who merely wish to take advantage of the facilities offered to gain a better knowledge of art.

Art Stores.—There are half a dozen stores in Detroit making a specialty of this line of goods, where almost everything can be obtained; and where anything is not in stock it can be readily secured for customers. Most of these stores are located on or near Woodward ave.

Art Stoves.—See stoves.

Artistic Furniture.—Detroit is the fortunate possessor of many factories and show rooms of these beautiful and useful articles, second to none in this country, in quality, workmanship, or price.

Artistic Silverware.—This city is rapidly coming to the front in this interesting and valuable art. No better instance could be mentioned than the beautiful solid silver punch bowl, made by a Detroit firm, and recently presented to the United States ship "Detroit."

Assessors, Board of.—The Board of Assessors is composed of three members appointed by the common council, on the recommendation of the mayor, who hold their office for the term of three years respectively, beginning on the first day of July, and shall devote their whole time to the service of the city in connection with the duties of their office, and the member whose term soonest expires shall be president of said board. It is the duty of the Board of Assessors, before the first day of April in each fiscal year, to assess, at its true cash value, all the real and personal property subject to taxation by the laws of this State, within the city, and make out and complete the assessment rolls, one for each ward, and also to make assessment roll for paving streets and alleys, and place the assessment on all street opening rolls. They shall cause notice to the tax-payers to be published in two daily newspapers, for two weeks prior to the first day of April in each year, that the assessment rolls have been completed. Any person considering himself aggrieved by reason of any assessment may complain thereof before said Board of Assessors, and, on sufficient cause being shown by such person to the satisfaction of such board, it shall review the assessment complained of, and may alter or correct the same. The Board of Assessors, or a majority of them, having completed the review and correction of said assessment rolls, shall sign on or before the third Tuesday in April in each year, and return the same to the common council. The common council, after receiving said rolls, shall, at its next regular session, proceed to consider the same, and any person considering himself aggrieved by the assessment of his property may appeal, in writing, to said common council, and they shall hear and determine all such appeals in a summary manner, and correct any errors which they may discover in the assessment rolls, and may increase or diminish any assessment as they may see fit. They may continue the consideration of the assessment rolls and the hearing of appeals for a period not exceeding sixteen days, after the time when they are first to be considered, and on or before the expiration of the sixteen days the assessment rolls shall be fully and finally confirmed by said common council. After the assessment rolls shall have been fully and finally confirmed the Board of Assessors shall cause the amount of all taxes in dollars and cents, authorized to be assessed and collected in each year, to be assessed ratably in the rolls for each ward in separate columns, showing the amount of city, school, highway and police taxes assessed to each person or lots in each year, and when said rolls are completed on July 1st each year the board shall turn said rolls over to the Controller and take his receipt therefor.

The city taxes are payable at the office of the Receiver of Taxes from July 1st to August 1st of each year, without percentage, after which time one per cent per month will be added thereto for six months, which becomes part of the tax, and thereafter runs with interest at the rate of ten per cent. per annum. If not paid before the first day of June following the property is sold for taxes.

Associated Press.—The Associated Press is an association of the principal newspapers in this country and Canada, organized for the purpose of gathering the news of the day. To most people the scope and aim of the association are a mystery. With agencies in all of the principal cities on this continent, and working in connection with similar organizations in Europe and elsewhere, the Associated Press is enabled to supply its members and clients with all the news of the world, on the same day on which it occurs.

In the United States the Associated Press has a telegraphic circuit which takes in all cities of importance. This circuit is manned with the most expert operators that are to be had, who receive all the matter from the wires right on a typewriter. Manifold copies, as many as are desired in each city, are taken, and every paper is supplied with copy that is ready for the printer to set up.

At each of the cities on the circuit a smaller report for the smaller papers in their respective district is made up, consisting of news specially interesting and affecting that particular section. The State of Michigan is served from Detroit, and all news originating within its confines is telegraphed to the Detroit agency, and from there given to the world.

The Detroit papers served by the Associated Press are the *Tribune*, *Free Press* and *Journal*. Charles E. Cutter, is manager of the Detroit agency, with offices at 325 and 326 Hammond Building.

Those daily papers, published in the city, which do not enjoy the Associated Press' privileges, are furnished with telegraphic news by the United Press.

Asylums.—See Benevolent Societies and Institutions.

Athletics.—Detroit enjoys the distinction of having several large athletic clubs and a number of smaller ones, which keep the public

CITY HALL.

Interested in legitimate sports of all kinds; there are also numerous private gymnasiums in different parts of the city, the principal clubs and athletic societies are:
Central Athletic Club.
Detroit Athletic Club.
Michigan Athletic Association.

Bankers.—The following is a list of private bankers doing business in Detroit:
Cameron Currie & Co., 82 Griswold street, second floor.
John L. Harper & Co., 82 Griswold street, first floor.
A. Ives & Son, 149 Jefferson avenue, cor. Griswold street.

Banks.—The following comprises a list of National and State or Savings Banks doing business in Detroit, with their location, capital, surplus and undivided profits, as follows:

NATIONAL BANKS.

American Exchange National Bank, cor. Griswold and Larned streets; capital, $400,000; surplus and undivided profits, $179,778.97.
Commercial National Bank, cor. Griswold and Larned streets; capital, $500,000; surplus and undivided profits, $254,172.30.
Detroit National Bank, cor Griswold and Congress streets; capital, $1,000,000; surplus and undivided profits, $286,125.59.
First National Bank, cor. Jefferson and Griswold streets; capital, $500,000; surplus and undivided profits, $226,354.26.
Merchants' and Manufacturers' National Bank, 91 Griswold street; capital, $500,000; surplus and undivided profits, $136,111.17.
Preston National Bank, 67 and 69 Griswold street; capital, $1,000,000; surplus and undivided profits, $96,748.79.

Third National Bank, cor. Griswold and Congress streets; capital, $300,000; surplus and undivided profits, $45,018.82.
Union National Bank, 143 Griswold street; capital, $200,000; surplus and undivided profits, $43,830.28.

STATE OR SAVINGS BANKS.

American Banking and Savings Association, 145 Griswold street; capital, $300,000; surplus and undivided profits, $41,547.84.
Central Savings Bank, 5 and 7 Campus Martius; capital, $100,000; surplus and undivided profits, $16,823.01.
Citizens' Savings Bank, 68 and 70 Griswold street; capital, $200,000; surplus and undivided profits, $116,568.78.
City Savings Bank, 147 Griswold street and 463 Gratiot avenue; capital, $250,000; surplus and undivided profits, $39,308.50.
Detroit Savings Bank, cor. Griswold and Larned streets; capital, $200,000; surplus and undivided profits, $359,125.55.
Detroit River Savings Bank, 14 Woodward avenue; capital, $100,000; surplus and undivided profits, $11,402.27.
Dime Savings Bank, cor Griswold and Michigan avenue; capital, $200,000; surplus and undivided profits, $44,710.09.
German American Bank, Monroe avenue and Cadillac square; capital, $100,000; surplus and undivided profits, $18,579.23.
Home Savings Bank, 151 Griswold street; capital, $200,000; surplus and undivided profits, $28,703.54.
McLellan & Anderson Savings Bank, 119 Griswold street; capital, $150,000; new bank opened May 23rd, 1893; no surplus.

Mechanics' Bank, 84 Griswold street; capital, $100,000; surplus, and undivided profits, $45,213.63.

Michigan Savings Bank, cor. Griswold street and Lafayette avenue; capital, $150,000; surplus and undivided profits, $65,716.79.

Peninsular Savings Bank, 40 Fort street west; capital, $500,000; surplus and undivided profits, $144,842.28.

People's Savings Bank, cor. Griswold and Fort streets; capital, $500,000; surplus and undivided profits, $198,258.25.

State Savings Bank, cor. Griswold and Fort streets; capital, $200,000; surplus and undivided profits, $129,398.15.

Wayne County Savings Bank, Congress street, near Griswold, capital, $150,000; surplus and undivided profits, $354,200.72.

Baptist Churches.—The following list gives the names and location of those in Detroit:

Clinton Avenue Baptist, southeast corner Jos. Campau and Clinton avenues.

Eighteenth Street Baptist, Eighteenth street, bet. Baker and Porter streets.

First Baptist, cor. Cass avenue and Bagg street.

First French Baptist, Sherman street, bet. Rivard and Russell sts.

First German Baptist, cor. Jos. Campau avenue and Arndt street.

North Baptist Church, cor. Woodward avenue and Boulevard.

Scotten Avenue Church, Scotten avenue.

Second Baptist Church (colored), Monroe avenue, bet. Brush and Beaubien streets.

Second German Baptist Church, cor. Linden and Eighteenth streets.

Shiloh Baptist Church (colored), 302 Columbia street east.

Twelfth Street Baptist Church, cor. Twelfth and Linden streets.

Warren Avenue Baptist Church, cor. Warren and Third avenues.

Woodward Ave. Baptist Church, cor. Woodward avenue and Winder streets.

Bar Library Association, of Detroit, was founded in 1856 for mutual advancement and benefit. The library contains about 12,000 volumes, relating exclusively to law, and is open to judges and members from 8 a.m. to 9 p.m. daily, except Sunday. There are at present 200 members; annual dues range from $5 to $40 Applicants admitted to the bar less than four years previous can become members for $5 annual dues, the fee being increased according to number of years in practice previous to application. The library is located on top floor of the Hammond building.

Baths.—A bath, either hot or cold, may be obtained at any first class barber shop, of which there are many located in all parts of the city, the usual price being 25 cents. There are also many places where one can get a Turkish, Russian, electric or mineral bath. Detroit also has a mineral spring, where baths may be obtained by either sex at convenient hours. At the Y. M. C. A. will be found a natatorium, which can be used winter or summer; but the most popular place in summer is in the bright, clear, blue water of the Detroit river. There are two private bath houses situated near the Belle Isle bridge approach, or if provided with a suitable costume anyone can go to Belle Isle Park and inquire of the first police officer the location of the bathing beach. There will soon be a suitable bath house erected on the island, as it is an improvement much needed.

Beggars.—Begging is not allowed in Detroit. Persons accosted on the street by a beggar should refer them to the McGregor Helping Hand Mission, where any honest person will receive aid; the Central Police Station also furnishes temporary lodging.

Belle Isle Park.—Is located opposite the eastern end of the city, at the head of the Detroit river, and is accessible by bridge or ferry boats which run every fifteen minutes from three different parts of the city during warm weather. The Island divides the water as it enters the river from Lake St. Clair into two streams, each about three-quarters of a mile wide. The island, which comprises about 750 acres, and is densely covered with magnificent old forest trees, was purchased by the city for the purpose of making it a park, and cost $200,000, and over $1,000,000 have already been spent in improving it; the city annually expending about $200,000 on it. In the park will be found beautiful driveways, walks, flowers, artificial canals and lakes, many fountains and artistic bridges, both iron and rustic, and for the lover of sport there are three base-ball diamonds, a one-mile race course, and a bicycle race course; there is also a large parade ground just in front of the artistic and useful casino; there is also an elegant skating pavilion for the use of skaters in winter, two large boat-houses containing hundreds of row boats for rent, and a large deer park.

Benevolent Societies and Institutions.—Detroit has always been noted for its generosity. No city of its size in the country can boast of more charitable institutions or of being quicker in replying to appeals for aid.

DETROIT HOME FOR BOYS, 172 High street west.

HOME FOR THE AGED POOR, corner Scott and Dequindre streets. In charge of the Little Sisters of the Poor.

HOME OF INDUSTRY FOR DISCHARGED PRISONERS from the State of Michigan, founded March 4th, 1888, by Mrs. Agnes L. D'Arcambal. The home is located at 259 Willis avenue east, which is about 1½ miles from the central part of the city. The men in the home are engaged in the manufacture of brooms, also caneing, painting and varnishing chairs. Visitors are given a cordial welcome at any time, and can be furnished with more information by calling at the home, address given above. Telephone, 4668, 2 rings. Orders for brooms, etc., promptly executed.

HOME OF THE FRIENDLESS ASSOCIATION, Warren avenue, west of Woodward avenue. The object of the association shall be to receive into a suitable home women and children of general good conduct and character who have been rendered homeless—or more than homeless—by want or distress. It is the intention of the home to help this class of unfortunates rather by prevention than reformatory measures, and to provide its inmates with a temporary home until they can be permanently placed, either as adopted children or domestics, with families of good moral character. A further object of the association is to endeavor to secure employment in respectable places for girls—strangers—who come to the city to seek service.

HOUSE OF PROVIDENCE, INFANT ASYLUM AND LYING-IN-HOSPITAL, corner St. Antoine and Elizabeth streets. Under charge of the Sisters of Charity. Organized, 1868.

LUTHERAN DEAF AND DUMB ASYLUM, is located in North Detroit, on Asylum road, about seven miles from the City Hall, and but a short distance from Detroit and Bay City R. R. and Grand Trunk R. R. It was organized in 1873. The founder was Dr. Speckhart, who was a deaf and dumb teacher in Germany for 20 years. It is managed by the Lutheran Society of Missouri Synod. There are now 40 children in the school, 120 having graduated. The articulation method is used to teach the pupils German, the parents being nearly all of that nation; it can be understood better than the finger language. English is taught in writing only.

OPEN DOOR SOCIETY, 223 Park street.

PROTESTANT ORPHAN ASYLUM, 988 Jefferson avenue.

ST. JOSEPH'S RETREAT FOR THE INSANE.—Dearborn. Owned and controlled by Sisters of Charity.

ST. VINCENT'S ORPHAN ASYLUM, McDougall avenue, between Larned and Congress streets. Was organized in 1851 and incorporated in 1871. It stood on the southwest corner of Larned and Randolph streets until the year 1875, when the new building on McDougall avenue was completed, and the orphans were brought there. The asylum now receives orphans, half orphans and destitute children between the ages of three and twelve years. The education imparted to the orphans is of a practical kind, and includes domestic work, besides the ordinary branches of a common school course.

SEAMAN'S HOME, located corner Griswold and Atwater streets, is an important institution for sailors, both morally and financially assisting sailors when sick or out of work, and bestowing other benefits.

THOMPSON HOME FOR OLD LADIES, corner Hancock and Cass avenues.

WOMAN'S HOSPITAL AND FOUNDLING'S HOME, Thirteenth street, two blocks south of Grand River avenues.

WORKING WOMAN'S HOME ASSOCIATION AND YOUNG WOMAN'S HOME, corner Clifford street and Adams avenues.

ZOAR ORPHAN ASYLUM AND HOME FOR THE AGED, 248 to 256 Harvey avenue.

Beth El Cemetery.—Located on Champlain street, and reached by Fort Wayne and Belle Isle Electric cars and owned by Beth El congregation; and sect. F north, in Woodmere cemetery, reserved for Beth El congregation.

Bicycling is a very popular and useful pastime in Detroit, on account of the many wide and beautiful streets and driveways, a proof of it being the thousands of riders of both sexes who are to be seen on the streets every day. The number is constantly increasing, as the city is rapidly putting in new and better pavements. Bicyclers are governed by the same rules as ordinary vehicles on paved streets during the day and evening, and are not allowed to ride on the sidewalks except on unpaved streets. On paved streets bicyclers are allowed to ride on the sidewalks after 11 p.m.

Bird and Dog Fanciers.—There are numerous private dealers in both birds and dogs. The principal dealer in birds, dog furnishings, etc., is located on Jefferson avenue, near Bates street. The principal dog kennel is located on Hastings street, near the boulevard.

Board of Trade.—The Board of Trade of the City of Detroit was first organized in 1856, and was sub-

BIRD'S-EYE VIEW FROM CITY HALL TOWER—LOOKING EAST

sequently incorporated under the General Act of the Legislature for the incorporation of commercial organizations, approved March 19, 1863. As provided in its constitution the object of the association shall be "to promote just and equitable principles in trade; to correct any abuses which may exist, and generally to advance the interests of trade and commerce, and promote the convenience and security of the members of the association." While the board is chiefly an exchange for the handling of grain and produce, it has always taken a deep interest in everything tending to promote the welfare of the city and the prosperity of its business enterprises. Its sympathy and aid has been cheerfully rendered towards the construction of new railroads throughout the State and tributary to Detroit; in the improvement of lake navigation, culminating in the successful issue of the great Deep Water Navigation Convention held in Detroit in December, 1891, for the securing of a 20 and 21 feet channel from the head of the lakes to Buffalo. A continuous and energetic interest has also been exhibited, touching questions relating to freight and transportation; the growth of manufacturing and mercantile industries, and like matters in commercial circles.

Since the organization of the board, its membership has included many of Detroit's most honored and successful citizens, while it has been so fortunate in its successive administrations in having officers willing to devote their best judgment and their experience to its general welfare. This is evidenced in the fact that the decisions of its tribunals have been of such force and wisdom that no member of the board has ever had a suit at law with another member in matters related to the board; neither has the association ever had any litigation with any of its members, although business transactions would reach scores of millions of dollars annually. Its receipts and shipments of grain during the past year have exceeded 20,000,000 bushels. This is a record few, if any, commercial or other associations in the country can show. The board is located on the third floor of Board of Trade Building, corner Jefferson avenue and Griswold street.

Boarding Houses are located in all parts of the city; prices range from $2.50 per week to the price of a good-sized income. Almost anyone can be suited at one of the numerous boarding house agencies, located principally on or near Griswold street.

Boating.—Detroit is famous for its beautiful river and Island Park. The latter contains numerous artificial lakes and canals, about 3 to 4 feet deep, which will accommodate hundreds of small boats without crowding. Boats can be obtained on the island for 10c. an hour, up. Access is had to the park either by bridge or one of the numerous and capacious ferry-boats, of which there are eight, which make regular trips to and from Windsor, Canada, and to and from Belle Isle, Woodward avenue, Twelfth street, and Jos. Campau avenue, at the uniform rate of 10 cents, round trip. There are also many excursion steamers run more or less regularly between different points of attraction up and down the river and lakes for many miles. There are also many places along the river and near the bridge approach where sail boats and yachts of all sizes can be hired by the hour, day or week. In addition to the above, thousands of boats of all sizes pass up and down the river annually, but as they nearly always take the south or Canadian channel, the north or American channel at Belle Isle is comparatively safe for small boats.

Boot Blacks may be found on all corners in the business centre of the city. The ordinary price for a shine is 5 cents. Boot rooms may be found at all hotels, where the price is generally 10 cents.

Boulevards.—See drives.

Bric-a-Brac. — Intending purchasers or visitors will find numerous establishments located on the main avenues, containing thousands of different articles of this kind.

Bridges.—Belle Isle Park bridge, connecting Detroit with its beautiful park, is 3,134 feet long, including approaches, and was built in 1887-88, and cost about $350,000. It is thrown across from the foot of Frontenac Boulevard, nearly at right angles with the channel, and 22 feet from the water to the bridge floor. There are 12 spans, a fixed span next the mainland, 156 feet long, then a pivot-draw span of 318 feet, followed by ten fixed spans, each of 156 feet. Each span consists of three trusses, each carrying a drive way 24 feet wide, and two sidewalks of 8 feet each. The draw-span is moved by steam power, and when open gives two passage-ways for vessels, each of 125 feet. There is also a new ornamental iron bridge over the Rouge River, on the Detroit River road, and several ornamental iron bridges and unique rustic bridges are to be found on Belle Isle Park.

Building Inspectors, Board of. —An Act of the Legislature, approved June 17, 1885, created a Board of Building Inspectors for the City of Detroit, which shall consist of three competent mechanics or architects, resident electors of the City of Detroit, to be appointed by the common council on the nomination of the Mayor, whose term of office shall be three years, who shall devote their entire time to the duties of their office, and who shall not be engaged or interested directly or indirectly in the building business, and shall be paid such salary for their services, under this Act, as the common council shall determine, but not to exceed $1,200 per annum. It is the duty of said building inspectors to make, at least once in each year, a thorough examination and inspection of all halls, opera houses, theatres, and buildings for amusement and recreation, school houses, churches, manufactories, workshops, stores, blocks for offices, hotels, boarding and tenement buildings, stands, platforms, freight or passenger elevators, and buildings or structures of every kind in the City of Detroit, used or intended to be used or occupied by gatherings of people, with reference to the safety of such buildings and structures for the purpose for which designed, and for the speedy and safe egress of the persons therein and thereon assembled, in case of sudden alarm or danger. In addition to such regular inspection of said buildings and structures it shall be the duty of said inspectors to promptly inspect any building or structure, of whatever character, when a complaint is made, or it comes to their knowledge that said building or structure is unsafe, and report in detail to the common council, at the end of each month, the work performed by them, and all information, with reference thereto, and shall submit to the said common council, in December of each year, a summary of their work of the preceding year. Also by Act of the Legislature, approved July 5, 1889, for the enforcement of the factory inspection laws, were placed in the hands of this board. And by a resolution of the council, March 13, 1888, the enforcement of the smoke ordinance was placed in the hands of the Board of Building Inspectors.

Catholic Club.—The Catholic Club, the leading Catholic social organization of Detroit, is located at the corner of Wilcox street and Library Place, one block from Woodward avenue and three blocks from the City Hall. The Club has a membership of 500, including leading business and professional men, manufacturers, bankers, journalists and lawyers, and its new stone club house at the above point has been occupied within the last two years. Prior to that time, the Club, which was organized in 1887, was located at First street and Lafayette avenue, where it outgrew its quarters and had forced on it the necessity of building the home it now occupies, at a cost of $70,000. The new house is a fully equipped home for the Club, containing reception halls and parlors, reading room, library, billiard parlors, bowling alleys, gymnasium and bath rooms, a music hall, card rooms, and other accommodations for the amusement and entertainment of its members.

Cemeteries.—The following comprises a list of the Cemeteries in and near Detroit, which find for further information under proper head. (Also see Crematory.) Beth El. Elmwood. Forest Lawn. Free Sons of Israel. German Lutheran. Mount Elliot. Mount Olivet. Shaary Zedeck. Woodmere.

Chamber of Commerce was organized January 5th, 1892. The matter had been under discussion for several years, as the want of a central commercial organization was clearly felt. The scope of the undertaking was to concentrate the various exchanges of the city, and to centralize their power and influence on all matters pertaining to the general interests of the city, while the different exchanges would still continue in their several legitimate fields of work. Much enthusiasm was displayed in its organization and the very best and most influential business and professional men in the city are numbered in its membership.

It having been clearly demonstrated by previous efforts that no organization formed to promote the public good could be held together without some financial basis for membership, it was determined to organize with a capital stock of $100,000, one thousand shares or memberships of $100 each. The yearly dues for 1892 and 1893 were fixed at $10. Early in the inception of the undertaking it was determined to erect for itself a building which, besides furnishing a large and commodious exchange hall and offices, should also become the home of the other exchanges, with a number of offices for rental purposes.

To this end a lot in the very heart of the city, being 88 feet on Griswold, and 100 on State, on the northeast corner of these two streets, was purchased, and plans in competition were made for a modern twelve-story structure, a cut of which is given

This building, now in process of erection, will be twelve stories high, fire proof, made of structural steel, with stone facings for the first five stories, and pressed brick and terra cotta above. Five elevators will make easy access to all parts of the building. The general Exchange Hall will be upon the third and fourth floors, two stories high, taking up about one-half of the space on these two floors. The offices will all be light and airy, either opening on the outside of the building or on the open court off from State street. As this is the first building of its kind to be erected in Detroit, much interest is felt in its construction. It will face westward upon Griswold street and a handsome little park, which will occupy the space made vacant by the burned high school building, built upon the old State Capitol site.

There are about 700 members in The Detroit Chamber of Commerce, standing fifth in point of membership in the Chambers of Commerce in the United States. It proposes, among other things, to do all it can to bring capital and deserving enterprises together, and to aid in securing suitable sites for new manufacturing plants. Its exchange rooms will afford ample facilities for the daily meetings of its members, and it will have the market reports from all parts of the world. The business men from different sections of the states who come frequently to Detroit, will find here comfortable office facilities and ready means for meeting the business men of Detroit of all classes and professions.

Its secretary will be ready at all times to answer legitimate letters of enquiry, and will welcome strangers to the city in search of information.

Christian Churches.—The following is a list of the names and location of those in Detroit:

CENTRAL CHRISTIAN CHURCH, corner Ledyard street and Second avenue.

DISCIPLES OF CHRIST, n. w. cor. Fourth and Plum.

Churches, of almost every denomination in the world, can be found in Detroit. Christian churches, of course, hold services on Sundays at the usual hours, 10 to 10:30 a.m., and 7 to 7:30 p.m. Sunday-school is held at nearly all the churches, usually about 2:30 p.m. Many churches also have meetings during the week. There are several synagogues in Detroit that usually hold services on Saturday. There are about 150 churches in Detroit, having a seating capacity of 200 to 2,000 each. The churches are, for the most part, supported by the regular congregation, with pew rents and voluntary contributions, but strangers are always welcome.

Churches, Miscellaneous—The following list embraces the principal places of worship not in fellowship with any other churches in the city:

ANGLICAN FREE CHURCH, cor. Woodward and Willis avenues.

CHURCH OF OUR FATHER (Universalist), Park street, west of Grand Circus Park.

CHURCH OF THE REDEEMER, cor. Holden and Fifth avenues.

DUTCH REFORMED, 318 Catherine street.

FIRST CONGREGATIONAL UNITARIAN, cor Woodward avenue and Edmund place.

FIRST GERMAN REFORMED ZIONS CHURCH, cor. Chene and Jay streets.

GERMAN EVANGELICAL ASSOCIATION, cor. Dubois and Catherine streets.

NEW JERUSALEM (Sweedenborgian), cor. Cass avenue and High street.

SACRED HEART OF MARY (Polish Catholic Reformed), cor. Canfield avenue and Russell street.

ST. PETER'S SCANDINAVISK LUTHERSKE KIRKE (Scandinavian), Catherine street, near St. Aubin avenue.

TRINITY CHURCH, cor Myrtle street and Trumbull avenue.

UNITY CHURCH (Undenominational Evangelical), cor. Brigham and Crawford streets.

CHAMBER OF COMMERCE BUILDING.
Corner Griswold and State Sts.

Citizens' Yachting Association.—Is one of the most active organizations on the lakes, and when anything is to be done every member feels that he is a committee of one to see that it is brought to a successful completion. In this manner the membership has grown to about 200, and the surplus to nearly $2,500. The club house is at the foot of McDougall avenue. It is a neat little building of two stories.

City Hall.—This was erected at a cost of $600,000, and was occupied for the first time on July 4th, 1871. It occupies the block bounded by Woodward ave., Michigan ave., Griswold street and Fort street, with an entrance on each of its four sides. It is a massive structure, five stories, and a tower of three stories high, from which an excellent view of the city can be had. It is used by the city and county governments. When built it was considered ample in size for 50 years or more, but so rapidly has the city grown that more room is imperative, and a new building worthy of the city will probably be started in the near future.

Clearing House Association.—Is located in the rear of the Citizens' Savings Bank, cor. Griswold and Larned streets, and was organized for the convenience of the various Detroit banks, who each send a clerk daily to represent them and transact their business.

Clubs—Of every kind and to suit every taste are to be found in Detroit. Following is a list of clubs, which speaks for itself:

Business Men's Cycle Club.
Catholic Club, cor. Wilcox and Barclay place.
Centennial Rowing and Athletic Association.
Central Athletic Club, Russell street, bet. Catherine and Sherman streets.
Citizens' Yachting Association.
City of the Straits Yachting Association.
Detroit Athletic Club.
Detroit Boat Club, boat house on Belle Isle Park.
Detroit Bowling Club, 512 Trumbull avenue.
Detroit Club, n. e. cor Cass and Fort streets.
Detroit Federation of Homing Pigeon Fanciers.
Detroit Fishing and Hunting Association.
Detroit Kennel Club.
Detroit Lantern Club.
Detroit Skating and Curling Club.
Detroit Wheelmen.
Detroit Woman's Club.
Detroit Yacht Club.
Detroit Social Turnverein.
East End Club.
Fort Gratiot Mutual Benefit Social Club.
Gentlemen's Club.
Interlaken Club.
Lake St. Clair Fishing and Shooting Club.
Lake Shore Fishing and Shooting Club.
Michigan Athletic Association.
Michigan Bowling Club.
Michigan Club.
Michigan Fishing and Shooting Association.
Michigan Kennel Club.
Michigan Yacht Club.
North Channel Shooting Club.
Old Reliable Rod and Gun Club.
Peoria Gun Club.
Phœnix Social Club.
Traveler's Club.
Turtle Lake Shooting Club.
Western Club.
West Side Club.
Yondotega Club.

Concerts.—Detroit people are noted for their musical taste and talent; in consequence there are always numerous concerts at the many places in and around Detroit, due notice of which is given in the papers.

Congregational Churches.—The following list gives the names and locations of those in the city:

CANFIELD AVENUE CONGREGATIONAL, cor. Canfield avenue and Hastings street.

FIRST CONGREGATIONAL, cor. Woodward and Forest avenues.

FORT STREET CONGREGATIONAL, Fort street west and Summit avenue.

MT. HOPE SUNDAY SCHOOL, 25th street, near Michigan avenue.

PLYMOUTH CONGREGATIONAL, cor. Trumbull avenue and Baker street.

WOODWARD AVENUE CONGREGATIONAL, cor Woodward avenue and Sibley street.

Consuls in Detroit:

BELGIUM.—Theophile Francois, 29 Hodges building.

COLOMBIA.—Herman Freund, 19 to 23 Monroe avenue.

DENMARK.—Peter Sorensen, 95 Woodward avenue.

FRANCE.—Joseph Belanger, consular agent, 94 Griswold street.

Coroners.—There are two coroners in Wayne county, their office being located in Detroit, cor. Clinton and Raynor streets. Each case of sudden death is at once reported to the nearest coroner, either by the attending physician or by the police, and an investigation is made if the coroner deems it advisable. A jury is paneled and an inquest is held, and if circumstances warrant it, an autopsy.

Correction, House of.—Among the institutions of the City of Detroit wide and favorably known, ranks our House of Correction, situated at the corner of Alfred and Russell streets, and is easily reached by Gratiot avenue cars. The original buildings of this prison were erected in 1860 and 1861, and cost, including additions since made, somewhat over $150,000. The total estimated value of land, buildings and appurtenances, in round numbers, foot up fully $500,000. The management and direction of the institution is vested in the Superintendent, under the control and authority of a Board of Inspectors, who are appointed by the common council, upon the nomination of the mayor. Said Board of Inspectors consists of four members, who serve without compensation. Quarterly statements and annual reports of the affairs of the House of Correction are required from the Board of Inspectors, and must be approved by the common council. The Board of Inspectors appoint the superintendent, whose term of office is three years.

County Clerk's Office is located on the first floor of the City Hall.

County Officers.—The principal officers of Wayne County are the sheriff, county treasurer, county clerk, register of deeds, and coroners. The location of their offices is given under the head of each.

County Treasurer's Office is located on the first floor of the City Hall

Crematory.—The Michigan Crematory is located on the south side of Lafayette avenue, between Springwells and West End avenues. It can be reached by the Fort street electric cars. The chapel is nicely furnished in hard woods, and will comfortably seat 100 persons. It contains a platform for the minister or speaker, and directly in front of the platform is a catafalque, on which the body is placed before it is gently lowered to the room below, where it is placed in a chilled steel crib, and then rolled into the retort which is heated to 2,500 degrees Fahrenheit. The body does not come in contact with the flames, as a good many suppose, but is placed in an oven in which the heat is so intense that it causes the body to change to dust in from one to two hours, according to the size of the body. The urn room is very handsomely and appropriately furnished, and already contains a good many beautiful urns. There is nothing harsh or gruesome about the whole process, that would jar even the most sensitive. It is one of the places of interest in Detroit, and a visit would amply repay any one, and perhaps remove prejudice against it.

Curious and Old Coins.—The principal dealer in these articles is H. Smith, on Gratiot avenue, near the Public Library. There are also fine collection in the Library Museum and the Art Museum.

Delray.—Is located just west of Detroit; in fact, a stranger can hardly tell where Detroit ends and Delray commences. There are numerous large factories located there. It has a population of 5,000, and is reached by both railroad and Fort Wayne electric cars.

Depots.—(See railways).

Des-Chree-Shos-Ka.—Is an island resort about eight miles down the river, formerly called Fighting Island; it was bought a few years ago by private parties and turned into a summer resort. The grounds are nicely laid out and there is an elegant hotel and casino on the island.

Detroit.—The City of Detroit has a history which is unique, romantic and thrilling. Few cities in any part of the new world have embraced, in their origin and progress, so many changes of government, such peculiar methods of administration, and so many social transformations. Detroit has been, by times, a trading-post, a military rendezvous, the scene of fearful massacres, the fitting-out place of bands of marauding savages, the abode of Acadian simplicity, the embodiment of early western activity, the exponent of self-satisfied conservatism, and the wide-spreading, widely known and enterprising metropolis of Michigan. It now literally sends the products of its laboratories and factories to every country on the globe, and to many islands of the sea. The number of persons employed in its factories and in the business enterprises naturally growing therefrom, does not, of itself, account for its increasing prosperity. The fact is, that a large proportion of its growth in recent years is because of its great attractiveness as a place of residence, and in this respect it has no rival on the continent, and possesses advantages that are impossible to other cities. Located on a river whose waters are of unrivaled purity, and whose entire length, of some twenty-seven miles, forms a natural harbor, beautified with more than a score of islands, it possesses a situation that is exceptional, and in the summer season especially, opportunities for recreation are numberless. The river never overflows its banks, is never violently agitated; the supply is limitless; it is usually placid and clear and affords superior ice. The size of the river and its strong and uniform current, together with the high banks, afford superior drainage facilities, which are well improved. The climate has enough of variety to give added zest to the seasons. The region is rarely, and never but for a few days at a time, subject to extreme changes of temperature. The autumns are especially pleasant, and the winters usually very mild. These and many other advantages unite to make the city emphatically a city of homes, and the United States census shows that in number of dwellings proportionate to population, it stands at the head of all cities of the country. Anyone who passes through the residence districts will see that the census statement is justified by actual facts. The beautiful effects of fine lawns and thrifty shade trees are seen in all parts of the city. Not only are its homes numerous, but many are surprisingly elegant and beautiful; and in business structures, as well, there are many that in any city would attract commendation.

Detroit Athletic Club, which has come to be the leading athletic organization of the west, was founded April 5th, 1887, it being the outcome of a small organization known for a number of years before as the Detroit Amateur Ball Club. The D. A. C. started in as a joint stock corporation with 500 shares at $10 each, and has already increased its membership to 1,000. The Athletic Club grounds, which consist of six acres, are the finest in the country, and are situated on Woodward avenue, in the heart of the finest residence portion of the city. The club house, although small, is a model of artistic beauty, and is most perfectly equipped in every particular, and for out-door exercise the club has most desirable facilities. The membership of the club is drawn from a class of young men between 18 and 25 years of age, and who are, taken as a whole, as fine a body of athletes as are to be found in the country. The club also has a number of young athletes in all branches, who are bound to make their mark in their respective lines.

Detroit Humane Society for the Prevention of Cruelty to Animals and Children, was organized November 5th, 1876, and has existed ever since; June 12th, 1877, the society was duly incorporated; in May, 1893, the society opened headquarters at room 21, Kanter building, making suitable arrangements for regular and effective work, and placing Mr. Vhay in charge. The society owns the only horse ambulance in Detroit. (See Horse Ambulance.)

Detroit Opera House.—Is located on the Campus Martius, and is a very popular place, nearly all strictly first-class plays being presented there.

Detroit Real Estate Board.—Within the past two years there has been a general movement among real estate dealers, in all the larger cities, to organize. Detroit dealers were among the last to respond to this tendency, but they finally fell into line, with the result that on December 20th, 1891, the Detroit Real Estate Board was organized. Starting with thirty-six (36) members, the board has steadily grown, until on June 1st, 1893, it comprised eighty-one (81) of the leading real estate dealers of the city. The same motives which prompt members of nearly every other profession and calling to maintain an organization, actuate real estate men to do the same. Among the objects sought to be attained by this board, in common with local boards of other cities, is the regulation of commissions in handling property, the en-

WOODWARD AVENUE—LOOKING NORTH.

couragement of honorable dealing among members and between members and patrons, the discountenancing of all schemes not in accord with legitimate and honorable business principles, and the cultivation of more friendly relations between members. The board also collects and publishes a large amount of information regarding Detroit, its advantages and resources, and encourages, in many ways, the location here of all enterprises and industries calculated to promote the advancement of the city. Through its public service committee, the board exerts its influence in favor of such state or municipal legislation as appears calculated to advance the city's interests, and opposes such legislation as seems inimical to the general good. The various local boards of the country, acting through the National Real Estate Association, work to secure, in the different States, uniformity of laws affecting the transfer, inheritance and encumbrance of real estate, also to simplify the mode of transfer. It is a further aim of both local and national boards to elevate the standard of real estate business and the *personnel* of those engaged in it. The office of the board is at 91 Griswold street.

Detroit Yacht Club has its club house opposite the driving park, and on the water's edge of the property lately offered to the city for a park. The club's anchorage is one of the best along the lakes, and the situation is such that the races open right into the free waters of Lake St. Clair.

Distances in Detroit.—The distance from the depots to the principal hotels, not located opposite the depots, is about ½ mile. From the city hall out Jefferson avenue to city limits is about 3½ miles, out Gratiot avenue about 4 miles, out Woodward avenue about 4 miles, out Michigan avenue about 4 miles, out Fort street west about 3½ miles. From city hall to waterworks about 5 miles, to Fort Wayne about 4 miles, to Grosse Pointe about 7 miles, to Belle Isle bridge about 3 miles.

Distances to Other Cities from Detroit:

	MILES.
New York, N. Y.	690
Buffalo, N. Y.	251
Niagara Falls, N. Y.	226
Chicago, Ill.	285
Kansas City, Mo.	708
St. Louis, Mo.	481
Indianapolis, Ind.	226
Cincinnati, O.	262
Cleveland, O.	173
Toledo, O.	60
Milwaukee, Wis., by rail	375
" " boat and rail	274
Toronto, Can	225
Montreal, Can.	558
Grand Rapids, Mich.	150
Saginaw, Mich.	97
Bay City, Mich.	108
Flint, Mich.	74
Port Huron, Mich.	60
Jackson, Mich.	76
Marquette, Mich.	442
Mackinac, Mich.	290

District Telegraph, American. —(See Messenger Service.)

Drinking Fountains.—Public drinking fountains for people are rather scarce, only one of any real value being in the city, that is the Bagley fountain, located near the City Hall, which cost $10,000. There are, however, numerous fountains for horses in different parts of the city, and the Humane Society provides and takes care of a number of stone tubs or jars for dogs.

Drives.—There are many pleasant drives in and about Detroit, those on Belle Isle Park being undoubtedly the finest. There are also many streets and avenues in the city which are very pleasant for a drive, including the new boulevard, which makes an entire circuit of the city. Many people like to drive to Grosse Pointe or out Woodward avenue, or out Fort street west, all of which make very enjoyable trips.

Drugs.—The fame of Detroit as a drug center far transcends any local or national boundaries. Its medicinal preparations are distributed over a domain upon which the sun never sets. The chief manufacturing enterprise of this kind is that of Parke, Davis & Co., possessing immense laboratories in Detroit and warehouses and offices for distributing purposes in New York, Kansas City and London, England, in addition to an auxiliary factory in Walkerville, Ont. Five travelers serve to guard their interests in Australia; they are also represented in India, South America and other places. A number of large enterprises in Detroit are devoted to the manufacture of specialities and non-secret remedies, the laboratory of Frederick Stearns & Co. being the largest of this class, with branches and representatives in New York, Windsor, Ont., London, England, India and New Zealand. Four travelers are kept busy in Australia and two in South America. The wholesale drug houses in our city are among the largest in the country, and through their numerous representatives patrol commercially a large section of the west. The largest jobbers of drugs and druggists' sundries are Messrs. Williams, Davis, Brooks & Co. In respect to capital invested and diversity of products, the drug interests of Detroit are easily the most extensive in the United States.

Dry Goods.—The principal retail stores are located on Woodward avenue, between Jefferson avenue and Grand Circus Park and tributary streets. The wholesale houses are located principally on Jefferson avenue, between the Michigan Central depot and Randolph street.

Education, Board of.—The school law of the city was so amended by an Act of the Legislature, approved March 6, 1889, as to change the composition of the board from twelve members, chosen from the city at large, to sixteen members, elected one by and from each ward, at the spring election held every alternate year, when judges of the supreme court are now required to be elected. The Act provided also that, at the spring election of the year 1889, one inspector for each ward should be elected; that those elected from the first, second, third, fourth, fifth, sixth, seventh and eight wards should hold office for two years; their successors should be elected for four years, and thereafter all members of said board should be elected for four years.

Electric Lights.—Detroit streets are lighted entirely by electricity, furnished by a private corporation, but the city has been given power to do its own lighting, and will probably do so in the near future. Belle Isle Park is also lighted by electricity, a plant being located on the island. Electric lights are also used in many stores and private residences.

Elmwood Cemetery.—Is located on Elmwood avenue, principal entrance at Monroe and Elmwood avenues. It is very beautifully laid out, and is well worth a visit. Fort Wayne electric cars pass it.

Episcopal Churches.—(See Protestant Episcopal Churches.)

Estimates.—A Board of Estimates was created by an Act approved June 24, 1887. It is constituted of two members from each ward, and five members from the city at large. They are elected at the same time and manner as the aldermen, and hold office for the same period. The members from the wards must have the same general qualifications as the aldermen. The five members at large are elected every alternate year. The members of the board receive three dollars as compensation for each daily session. The ex-officio members of the board are the President and Chairman of the Committee on Ways and Means of the Common Council, the City Controller, City Counselor, President of Board of Education, Board of Water Commissioners, Board of Police Commissioners, Board of Poor Commissioners, President of Fire Commissioners, the senior members of Board of Inspectors of the House of Correction, and of the Board of Public Works. The ex-officio members have the right of participation in the deliberations of the board, but cannot vote. The board elect a president from their members, and the city clerk is ex-officio the Secretary of the board. The board must act upon the general city estimates and all other measures for the raising of money, whether by tax, levy, or by the issuing of bonds. The board may decrease or disapprove, but cannot increase the amount proposed to be raised. Only the amount approved by the Board of Estimates can be raised.

Evangelical Lutheran Churches.
—The following list gives the names and location of those in Detroit:

GERMAN.

BETHANIA CHURCH, corner Meldrum and Pulford avenues.

BETHLEHEM CHURCH, McKinstry avenue, bet. Fort street and Dixon.

BETHEL CHURCH, cor. Dubois street and Medbury avenue.

CHRIST CHURCH, n. w. cor. Twenty-sixth and Myrtle streets.

CHRIST CHURCH, cor. Scotten and Wolff avenues.

EMANUEL, cor Seventeenth and Pine streets.

EMMAUS' CHURCH, cor. Twelfth and Lysander streets.

GETHSEMANE CHURCH, west side Twenty-eight street, north of Buchanan.

HOLY CROSS, cor. Jos. Campau avenue and Illinois street.

ST. JAMES', cor. Poplar and Humboldt avenues.

ST. JOHN'S CHURCH, cor. Maybury Grand avenue and Poplar st.

ST. LUKE'S, cor. Field and Kercheval avenues.

ST. MATTHEW'S, Congress and Rivard streets.

ST. PAUL'S CHURCH, cor. Jos. Campau avenue and Jay street.

ST. PETER'S, 219 Pierce street.

SALEM CHURCH, cor. Chene and Bellair streets.

STEPHANUS', cor. Chamberlain and Lawndale avenues.

TRINITY, cor. Gratiot avenue and Rivard street.

ZION CHURCH, 555 Welch avenue.

Evangelical Protestant Churches.—The following list gives the names and locations of those in Detroit:

GERMAN.

ST. JOHN'S, Russell street, bet. Antietam and Chestnut streets.

ST. JOHN'S MISSION, Harper

avenue, bet. St. Aubin avenue and Dubois street.

ST. JOHN'S, cor. Burdeno avenue and Moore street, Delray.

ST. MARCUS', cor. Dix and Military avenues.

ST. PAUL'S, cor. Seventeenth and Rose streets.

Exchanges.—Following is a list of Detroit exchanges. Special mention of each will be found in their proper alphabetical order:
Board of Trade.
Chamber of Commerce.
Detroit Real Estate Board.
Merchants' and Manufacturers' Exchange.
Produce Exchange.

Excursions—To and from Detroit are very frequent during the summer months, ranging from a trip to Belle Isle Park to a trip of a hundred miles or more, by boat or rail, besides the excursions given, at irregular intervals, by various societies, etc. There are many regular steamers plying between Detroit and adjacent points, which are patronized as much for pleasure as for business. The principal excursion points are:
Belle Isle Park.
Des-Chree-Shos-Ka.
Flats (St. Clair).
Grande Pointe.
Oak Grove.
Orchard Lake.
Orion Lake.
Put-in-Bay.
Star Island.
Sugar Island.
And many other places.

Express Offices.—A package can be shipped from Detroit to almost any part of the world by express, most of the large express companies having an office in Detroit or an agreement with the companies which reach here. The following comprises a list of the companies doing business in this city:

AMERICAN EXPRESS CO., 86 Woodward avenue.

DOMINION EXPRESS CO., 104 Woodward avenue.

NATIONAL EXPRESS CO., 6 Monroe avenue.

NORTHERN PACIFIC EXPRESS CO., 6 Monroe avenue.

PACIFIC EXPRESS CO., 104 Woodward avenue.

RIVER ST. CLAIR EXPRESS CO., foot Griswold street.

UNITED STATES EXPRESS CO., 104 Woodward avenue.

WELLS, FARGO & CO., 86 Woodward avenue.

Ferry Boats.—Detroit now has a very fine fleet of ferry boats, and there is no other city in the world where so much can be had for so little money, and the hundreds of thousands of people who patronize them annually is proof of this fact. See time table below:

WEEK DAYS.

First boat leaves Windsor 6.00 a.m.
"   "   "   Detroit 6.15 "
Every 15 minutes to 7 a. m.
Then every 10 minutes to 8.00 p.m.
"   " 15   "   10.15 "
"   " 20   "   11.50 "
(Last boat from Detroit.)
Last boat from Windsor 11.40 p. m.

SUNDAY.

First boat leaves Windsor at 7.00 a.m.
"   "   "   Detroit 7.10 "
Then every 20 minutes to 9.30 "
"   " 15   "   2.00 p.m
"   " 10   "   8.00 "
"   " 15   "   10.15 "
"   " 20   "   11.30 "
(Last boat from Detroit.)
Last boat from Windsor 11.20 p. m.

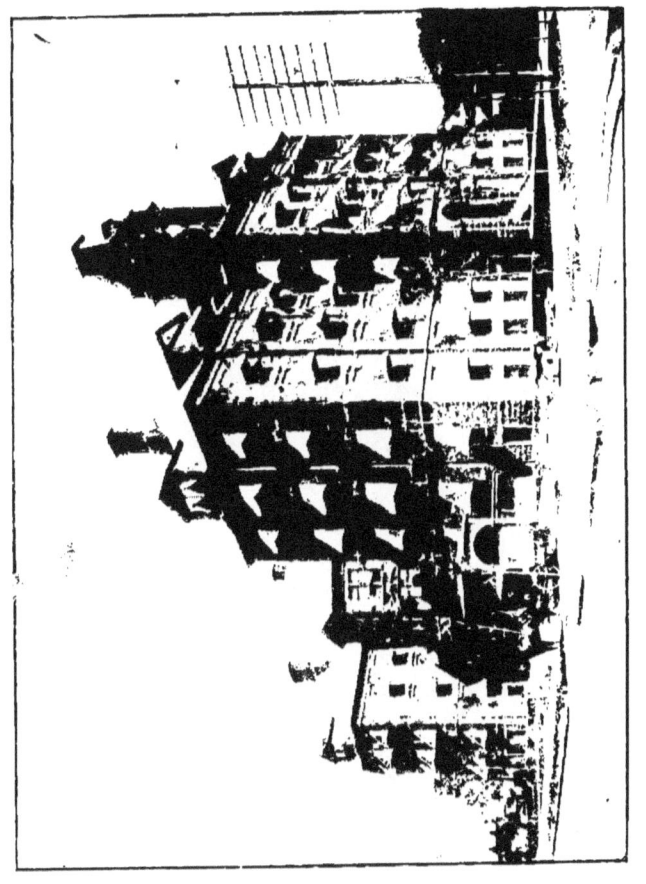

GRACE HOSPITAL.
(Cor. John R. St. and Willis Ave.

DES-CHREE-SHOS-KA.
At 10 a.m., 11.40 a.m., 1.20, 3.00, 4.40, 6.20, 8.00 and 9.20 p. m. Fare, round trip, 15c.

BELLE ISLE PARK.
Boat every 20 minutes from 9.30 a. m. to 10.30 p. m.

Fire Department.—The fire department is under the control and management of the Fire Commission, a board composed of four members, created by act of the Legislature. The said commissioners having control and management of all officers, men, property, measures and action for the prevention and extinguishment of fires within the city of Detroit, and empowered and directed to possess and exercise fully and exclusively all the powers, and perform all the duties for the government, management, maintenance and direction of the fire department.

The terms of office of the commissioners are four years, one expiring each year. They are appointed by the common council on the nomination of the mayor. The fire commissioners receive no pay for their services, the office being purely honorary and non-partisan.

The commission was organized April 1, 1867, since which time the fire department has been under its control and management.

The fire department comprises the following apparatus: Eighteen steam fire engines, manned and equipped, one of these being a marine company or fire-boat; six chemical companies, manned and equipped; eight hook and ladder trucks, manned and equipped; five supply wagons.

IN RESERVE, WITHOUT COMPANIES.—One first-class steam fire engine and equipment; two second-class steam fire engines and equipment; two hose carts equipped with hose; one hose wagon equipped with hose. This apparatus is kept in readiness for instant use.

Fire Insurance.—Detroit has the lowest rate of fire insurance of any city in the United States. This is undoubtedly owing to a large extent to the excellent fire service, which is second to none in the world. Rates of insurance for business places range from 75c. to $1 per hundred yearly, and for residences from 40c. to 50c. per hundred for three years.

Fish Hatchery (United States)— Is located at the cor. of Jos. Campau avenue and Champlain street, and is open to visitors from 10 a. m. to 4 p. m. Fort Wayne electric cars pass it.

Fishing.—Persons fond of this sport can find plenty to occupy their time in Detroit river or Lake St. Clair. The flats, in Lake St. Clair, is one of the greatest fishing places in this country, and is easily reached in a few hours' ride.

Fishing Clubs.—Most Detroiters are very much interested in fishing, but the fame of Detroit and vicinity, as regards fishing, has grown to such proportions that it has been practically impossible to confine the membership of fishing clubs to Detroit and vicinity, many of the members of Detroit clubs living from 50 to 1,000 miles from Detroit. The principal clubs are:

Detroit Fishing and Hunting Association.
Interlaken Club.
Lake St. Clair Fishing and Shooting Club.
Lake Shore Fishing and Shooting Club.
Michigan Fishing and Shooting Association.
Old Reliable Rod and Gun Club.

Flats (St. Clair)—Is located about 20 miles from the head of the Detroit river, and is a very popular hunting and fishing resort. Many fine club houses, summer hotels and private residences are erected there.

Flowers—Are never scarce in Detroit, as there are several large green-houses located here; to say nothing of the many private conservatories. The majority of those who own green-houses have a down town office or conservatory, where flowers of all kinds and for all occasions may be obtained. The address of the principal ones of these is: John Breitmeyer & Sons, cor. Gratiot and Miami avenues; Detroit Floral Co., John R. street, near Harper Hospital; B. Schroeter, Elmwood avenue and Champlain street. The cheaper class of flowers may be found in abundance at the different markets.

Forest Lawn Cemetery.—This is the newest of the Protestant cemeteries, and is intended to meet the needs of the northern and eastern portions of the city. The cemetery is located on the line of the Grand Trunk Railway and the Norris Plank road, 5½ miles from the City Hall. It comprises 100 acres of land, admirably suited for the purpose. The land is rolling, and about half of it is covered with small trees and shrubbery. Diagonally across the grounds runs a brook with high banks, which will furnish unsurpassed vault sites. A gothic entrance building and a vault have been erected. A cindered and graveled driveway is completed entirely across the grounds. The projectors are confident that the public will agree with them in thinking that the best possible location for a cemetery has been chosen, and that the work that has been put upon the grounds is thorough and in good taste.

Fort Wayne—Is located four miles west of the city hall, on the bank of the Detroit river, and is reached by Fort Wayne electric cars. It is a picturesque and interesting place to visit; from its elevated ramparts an elegant view of the river and shipping can be obtained; opposite is the ancient village of Sandwich, Can., and looking up the river (to the east) one can see Windsor and Walkerville, Can., and at the head of the river, some eight miles away, can be dimly seen the beautiful Belle Isle park, set in the centre of the river like an emerald in blue enamel.

Freemasonry.—The headquarters of Freemasons in Detroit are at the Consistory on Lafayette avenue, near First street, and in the Wayne County Savings Bank building, Congress street west, near Griswold street. Meetings are held every evening except Saturday at both places.

Free Sons of Israel Cemetery.—Located on Section E, Woodmere cemetery, and owned by the Society of Free Sons of Israel. (See Woodmere cemetery.)

Furniture.—Few cities in the United States offer equal advantages for purchasing furniture as Detroit, situated as it is so near the great furniture manufacturing centre, and possessing several furniture factories, which are second to none. Furniture may be purchased for cash, or on weekly or monthly payments, on any of the principal avenues.

Gas—Is furnished Detroit and vicinity by the Detroit Gas Co., office located on Congress street west, near Griswold street. The company furnishes meters, requiring a small deposit from strangers for the use of the same. The price for illuminating gas is $1.25 per 1,000 feet, and for natural or fuel gas 29 7-10 cents per 1,000 feet.

Grace Hospital.—Was incorporated November 28, 1888; opened for patients December 6th, 1888. The worthy poor of Detroit, if not incurable or contagious, are treated free. Visitors are welcomed on Tuesdays and Fridays, 2.00 to 4.00 p.m., and on Sundays from 1.15 to 3.15 p.m. There is an ambulance and free dispensary connected with the hospital.

Grand Circus Park—A public park of about six acres, bounded by Park street, Witherell street, Adams avenue, and Woodward avenue running through the centre. The park itself abounds with fine shade trees, has two fountains, and in summer is a pleasant and favorite place, with residents and strangers stopping in the vicinity. The Woodward avenue electric cars pass it.

Gratiot Avenue—Is one of the main arteries of business in Detroit. It is crowded with people and vehicles of all kinds from early morning until late in the evening.

Grosse Isle—Is beautifully situated on the American side of the main channel of the Detroit river, and is about 7½ miles in extreme length, with an average breadth of about 1½ miles, and contains about 10 square miles, or 6,400 acres. The river below the island is some four miles wide, opening out into Lake Erie, six miles away. The cooling breezes of lake and river, together with its arrable soil and the vernal shade of native trees, make this an ideal spot for summer homes. Many of the substantial men of Detroit spend their summer here.

Grosse Pointe—Is located about 7 miles out Jefferson avenue, and has a number of fine summer residences, which were built and are occupied by wealthy Detroiters.

Hack Fares.—The drivers or owners of public conveyances may demand and receive, for conveying passengers, the following rates or prices of fare, and no more, to wit: For carrying a passenger from one place to another, within the limits of said city, 50 cents; children under ten years of age, not exceeding two in number, when accompanied by parents or guardians, shall be carried free of charge; those in excess of that number shall each be charged half fare For the use of any public conveyance by the hour, for not more than four persons, and with the privilege of going from place to place, and stopping as often as required, $1.50 per hour for the first hour, and $1 for each additional hour, and for fractional hours at the rate of $1 per hour, and for each additional passenger, 25 cents per hour; for the use by the day of such conveyance, $5; for each trunk, 15 cents; but no charge shall be made for any bag, valise, or bundle, weighing less than 50 pounds. When a public conveyance is used between the hours of 11 p.m. and 5 a.m. it shall be lawful to demand and receive, for the same services, one-half more than the rates prescribed above. Any disagreement as to time and rates shall be determined by the mayor.

Halls.—The following list gives the names and location of the principal halls in the city:

ABSTRACT BUILDING, s. s. Lafayette avenue, bet. Griswold and Shelby street.

ARBEITER HALL, cor. Russell and Catherine streets.

AUDITORIUM, n. s. Larned street, bet. Bates and Randolph streets.

BEECHER'S HALL, 242 Jefferson avenue.

BOHEMIAN TURNER HALL, cor. Calhoun and St. Antoine streets.

CHENE HALL, 686 Monroe ave.

CLAWSON'S HALL, 96 Miami ave.

COLOMBO HALL, 285 Gratiot ave.

EAST SIDE TURN-VEREIN HALL, 728 Chene street.

FAFEYTA'S OPERA HOUSE, 996 Michigan avenue.

FRATERNITY HALL, cor. State street and Park place.

GERMAN SALESMEN'S HALL, 87 and 89 Monroe avenue.

GERMANIA HALL, cor Russell and Mullett streets.

HARMONIE HALL, cor. Champlain and Beaubien streets.

MORETON'S HALL, 331 and 333 Michigan avenue.

PHILHARMONIC HALL, cor. Lafayette avenue and Shelby street.

STRASSBURG'S DANCING ACADEMY, Adams avenue east, near Woodward avenue.

TINNETTE'S HALL, 310 Rivard st.

Harbor.—Detroit undoubtedly has a harbor as fine as any in the world, comprising as it does the entire Detroit river, over twelve miles long and one mile wide.

Harper Hospital.—Is located on John R. street and Martin place. It is one of the largest hospitals in the city, with accommodations for hundreds of patients. Adjoining it is the Farrand Training School for nurses.

Health Department.—The Board of Health of the city of Detroit was organized under an act of the Legislature, approved May 26, 1881, and consists of three practicing physicians, appointed by the common council on the nomination of the mayor, controller, and president of the Metropolitan Police Commission, who are ex-officio members.

The Board of Health, thus constituted for the purpose of organization and management of its department, shall have authority of other boards in said city, and ordinarily pertaining to such bodies, . . . and also to appoint a secretary, as an executive officer, who shall be known as the health officer of said city. Office located in Municipal Building, cor. Clinton and Raynor streets. (See Milk Inspector.)

Horse Ambulance.—No part of the work of the Humane Society is of more importance to the public than the prompt and immediate relief and removal of sick and injured horses from the streets to some place where they can be cared for. For this purpose the society has had built an ambulance expressly for sick and injured horses. Subscribers may use the ambulance whenever necessary without charge, except the subscription fee, which is quite small. Non-subscribers must pay for each time the ambulance is used. (See cut of Ambulance in this book.)

Horse Show.—The Detroit Riding Club gave a very elite and successful exhibition recently, which has placed Detroit in the front rank in this form of exercise.

Hospitals, Dispensaries, etc.— The following list gives the names and locations of those in Detroit:

CHILDREN'S FREE HOSPITAL, 336 Fort street west, cor. Seventh street.

DETROIT EMERGENCY HOSPITAL AND FREE DISPENSARY, Porter street, cor. Michigan avenue and Second street.

HORSE AMBULANCE.

DETROIT SANITARIUM, 250 Fort street west.
GRACE HOSPITAL, cor. John R. street and Willis avenue.
HARPER HOSPITAL, John R. street, head of Martin place.
ST. LUKE'S HOSPITAL AND CHURCH HOME, Fort street west, cor. McKinstry avenue.
ST. MARY'S FREE EYE AND EAR INFIRMARY, Clinton street, near St. Antoine street.
ST. MARY'S HOSPITAL, St. Antoine street, bet. Clinton and Mullett streets.
UNITED STATES MARINE HOSPITAL, s. w. cor. Jefferson and Mt. Elliott avenues.

Hotels.—First-class hotels are not numerous in Detroit, but are famous for their great capacity and beauty of furnishing. The principal ones run on the American plan are the Hotel Cadillac, Michigan and Washington avenues; the Russell House, Woodward avenue and Fort street, and the Wayne Hotel, opposite M. C. R. R. depot. The principal one run on the European plan is the new hotel Ste. Claire, Monroe avenue and Randolph street. Prices for the above range from $2.00 to $10.00 per day, according to location and number of rooms. There are also many smaller hotels in different parts of the city, some run on the American and some on the European plan, at which prices range from $1.00 per day up. Following is a list of hotels doing business in Detroit:

AVENUE HOUSE, 252 Woodward avenue.
CASS AVENUE HOTEL, cor. Cass avenue and Lewis street.
FRANKLIN HOUSE, cor. Larned and Bates streets.
GIES'S EUROPEAN HOTEL, 10-14 Monroe avenue.
GRIFFIN HOTEL, cor. River and Third streets.
HOTEL CADILLAC, 50-78 Michigan avenue.
HOTEL GOODMAN, 22-26 Grand River avenue.
HOTEL LIEDERS, cor. Randolph and Larned streets.
HOTEL NORMANDIE, 11-23 Congress street east.
HOTEL RENAUD, 128 Grand River avenue.
HOTEL RICHTER, 11-13 State street.
PERKINS' HOTEL, 100 Grand River avenue.
RANDOLPH HOTEL, 178 Randolph, cor. Champlain.
RICE'S HOTEL, 223 Jefferson avenue, cor. Randolph street.
RUSSELL HOUSE, cor. Woodward avenue and Cadillac square.
STE. CLAIRE HOTEL, cor. Monroe avenue and Randolph street.

Humane Society.—(See Detroit Humane Society.)

Jail.—(See Wayne County Jail).

Jefferson Avenue.—Is one of the widest and handsomest streets in Detroit; the lower part is given up entirely to wholesale business houses, but after passing St. Antoine street the visitor will find only elegant churches and residences, with fine old shade trees gracing their front for miles.

Jewish Synagogues.—The following list gives the names and locations of those in Detroit:

BETH EL TEMPLE, cor. Washington avenue and Clifford street.
BETH JACOB, cor. Montcalm and Hastings streets.

Bnai Israel, Mullett street, bet. Hastings and Antoine.

Shaary Zedeck, cor. Congress and St. Antoine streets.

Labor Organizations.—Like all large cities where there are a number of trades unions, Detroit has fallen into line, and has its council of trades and labor unions. The present trades council, as it is commonly known, was organized in 1880, when a few earnest workers among the trades people started the movement for a central body of trades. Little did the founders dream that their modest initiative would lead to such a powerful organization as it is to-day. Nor did they imagine that the organization would assume the functions of a body having for its object the promotion of union principles in general, organizing and championing the interests of the wage workers, and elevating their condition morally, intellectually and socially.

In 1865 a central body, called the Trades Assembly, was organized, but disbanded in 1878 A year later it was re-organized under the name of the Labor League. This was also short lived, and in 1880 the present council was organized.

Like most labor organizations many obstacles were encountered. It started with nine unions and increased to twenty, when it became popular to belong to the Knights of Labor, and the roll came down to seven unions.

It soon became evident, however, that open organization was the best form of a working-class organization, and the different unions surrendered their K. of L. charters, and once more became trade unions.

Within the last few years the council has grown rapidly, and at the present time there are 40 distinct and separate unions connected with it, representing, at a low estimate, over 10,000 organized workingmen. The council is also affiliated with the American Federation of Labor and the Michigan State Federation of Labor.

The council now has a large and commodious hall in the Hilsendegen block on Monroe avenue, handsomely furnished, together with a library. All the daily papers are on file, and also the various labor papers and industrial journals and leading magazines. This room is open to the members of the various unions and also to the public generally.

The oldest labor organizations in the council are the printers, iron molders and cigarmakers. They also rank the largest in membership. The meetings of the council are held every alternate Thursday, and are open to the public. The press of the city also give good and accurate accounts of the deliberations. It may not be amiss to say that the delegates always take a lively interest in public affairs, and fearlessly champion the rights of the masses in all questions affecting their welfare in municipal and state affairs, and keep their respective unions posted in such matters. They are also unflinching in their support of and loyalty to the principles of unionism.

The Central Labor Union of the city comprises the German labor organizations, who also have done much towards bettering the condition of the working classes.

Leesville—Is located about six miles out Gratiot avenue, and is reached by street cars from Detroit.

Licenses—Are issued by the mayor, after receiving a certificate from the secretary of the Metropolitan police that the fees therefor are paid.

Lodgings.—(See Rooms.)

Lutheran Cemetery, situated on Mt. Elliott avenue, and about four miles from city hall. Gratiot avenue or Belt Line cars run within easy reach of same.

Lyceum Theatre.—Is located cor. Randolph and Champlain streets, and is a very neat and cosy place to spend an evening. There is nearly always some standard play on the board during the season.

Manufactures. — Detroit now literally sends the products of its laboratories and factories to every country on the globe, and to many islands of the sea. In several mercantile lines it is a larger producer than any other city. Of stoves, cars, pharmaceutical preparations and seeds, it markets more than is produced in any other city, and in the manufacture of furniture and chairs, safes, pins, tobacco, organs, white lead, oils, varnishes, matches and pearl buttons, it is, possibly, not second to any other manufacturing center. Other manufactures are iron and steel, steam engines and boilers, mill machinery, leather, boots and shoes, clothing, trunks, billiard tables, lumber, hoops, staves and heading, ale, beer and malt, and a good many other articles. These facts clearly indicate its importance and prosperity as a leading labor centre, and the output of its factories increases steadily from year to year.

Marine Hospital (United States) —Is located cor. Jefferson and Mt. Elliott avenues.

Markets.—Central market is under the control of the city, on the block bounded by Cadillac square, Bates and Randolph streets. Stalls which may become vacant for any reason whatever are leased by permit to the first eligible applicant without other charge than the rental. Market wagon stands are located as follows:

CENTRAL MARKET, in rear of Market building.

EASTERN MARKET, on Russell and Market streets, bet. High and Adelaide streets.

WESTERN MARKET, on Michigan avenue and Eighteenth street.

Masonic Temple.—(See Freemasonry.)

Medical Associations and Colleges.—The following list gives the names of those in Detroit:

COLLEGE OF PHYSICIANS AND SURGEONS OF MICHIGAN.—Meets first Tuesday of each month at Hotel Normandie.

DETROIT ACADEMY OF MEDICINE.—Organized, 1869. A society of physicians and surgeons for mutual professional improvement and cultivation of harmony among its fellows.

DETROIT COLLEGE OF MEDICINE.—Cor. St. Antoine and Mullett streets.

DETROIT MEDICAL AND LIBRARY ASSOCIATION.—Meets every Monday at Cowie building, cor. Gratiot avenue and Farrar street.

MICHIGAN COLLEGE OF MEDICINE AND SURGERY, 7-9 Porter street.

Merchants' and Manufacturers' Exchange.—The Merchants' and Manufacturers' Exchange of Detroit was organized in 1878, and has grown to be one of the most important business associations in the west. The organization was completed on the 26th day of March, in the year named, 82 members signing the constitution on that day. Since that time the Exchange has so increased that it now numbers among its members a very large proportion of the manufacturers and jobbers of Detroit. It has not only kept pace with the commercial growth of Detroit, but has constantly gone in advance and so prepared the way that the business of the city might reach out to new fields by new methods.

The objects of the Exchange are many. It seeks to maintain a high and exact standard of business morality among the thousands of dealers who buy in Detroit, and to guard against fraud and imposition.

By the interchange of information among its members they are informed of any tardiness, irregularity, neglect, or positive dishonesty on the part of any customer of an individual member. As nearly every merchant in the whole region tributary to Detroit has dealings with members of the Exchange, this serves to give a system of reporting more exact and reliable than is possible for a commercial agency to supply. It is not only toward delinquent buyers that the efforts of the Exchange is directed. It is quick to recognize good business qualities and honorable business methods and to protect and advertise the credit of buyers who deal exactly and pay promptly. Thus it is as valuable to the reliable retailer as it is to its own members, and tends on every hand to foster a healthy and liberal trade spirit.

However important this system may be, it is not the only, nor the broadest function of the Exchange. Nothing of importance to the interests of Detroit is foreign to its aims. It takes the lead in working against unjust discrimination on the part of common carriers, and has done more than any other agency to secure equitable rates for Detroit merchants, from the railroads entering the city. It is always interested in securing the construction of new railroads, where such are needed and seem likely to favor the interests of Detroit merchants. It has also done good service in breaking combinations of insurance companies, made to exact excessive premiums, and has everywhere arrayed itself against every fraud and imposition which attacks the business interests of the city.

Two results have followed from the work of the Exchange: first, the manufacturers and jobbers of the city have found that they cannot afford to do without the assistance and protection it gives; second, the various schemes which formerly bled business men as individuals have found that they cannot do so when united in so strong a combination. To defy the Merchants' and Manufacturers' Exchange is to throw down the glove to the combined capital, shrewdness and determination of the business men of Detroit, and even a railroad or insurance pool would hesitate to do that.

Messenger Service.—This is divided into three classes in Detroit. The Western Union Telegraph Co. employ 35 boys, and the Postal Telegraph Co. employ 25 boys for the exclusive purpose of gathering and delivering telegrams. The American District Telegraph Co. employ 20 boys for service of all kinds, from calling for or delivering a parcel to escorting a lady. Messengers can be summoned by telephone or messenger call boxes, which are to be found in most large business places. The post office authorities employ 8 boys for the delivery of letters having an immediate delivery stamp attached.

Methodist Episcopal Churches. —The following list gives the names and location of those in Detroit:

ARNOLD M. E. CHURCH, cor. Seventeenth and Buchanan streets.

ASBURY M. E. CHURCH, cor. Ferry avenue and Dubois street.

BALDWIN AVENUE M. E. CHURCH, cor. Baldwin avenue and Champlain street.

CASS AVENUE M. E. CHURCH, cor. Cass and Selden avenues.

CENTRAL M. E. CHURCH, cor. Woodward and Adams avenues.

FIRST GERMAN M. E. CHURCH, cor. Jos. Campau avenue and Heidelberg street.

HAVEN M. E. CHURCH, cor. Sixteenth and Bagg streets.

HUDSON AVENUE M. E. CHURCH, Hudson avenue, west of Maybury Grand avenue.

LINCOLN AVENUE M. E. CHURCH, cor. Lincoln and Putnam avenues.

MARY W. PALMER M. E. CHURCH, cor. McDougall avenue and Champlain street.

NINDE M. E. CHURCH, cor. Twenty-eighth and Visger streets.

PRESTON M. E. CHURCH, cor. Twenty-third and Lambie place.

SECOND GERMAN M. E. CHURCH, Sixteenth street, near Michigan avenue.

SIMPSON M. E. CHURCH, cor. Grand River avenue and Sixth street.

TABERNACLE M. E. CHURCH, cor. Howard and Fourth streets.

THIRTY-SECOND STREET M. E. CHAPEL (German), west Thirty-second street, near Michigan avenue.

WELCH AVENUE M. E. MISSION, Welch avenue.

WOODWARD AVENUE M. E. CHURCH, cor. Woodward and Harper avenues.

Michigan Athletic Association—Is one of the many popular and successful clubs in Detroit. It has an elegant home and grounds of its own at the corner of Elmwood avenue and Congress street.

Michigan Avenue—Is one of the leading business streets of Detroit, being lined on both sides for miles with retail stores of every description.

Michigan Club.—The Michigan Club, cor. Fort and Wayne streets, was organized in 1885 for the purpose of aiding the Republican party in this State, in the maintenance of its power, extension of its principles, and for the purpose of elevating politics and keeping political work upon a high plane. The work is done in the main by the distribution of literature, holding of meetings for the discussion of political questions, and giving, once in each year, a banquet to which prominent Republican leaders of the nation are invited and asked to speak upon the leading issues of the day. The club numbers in the neighborhood of 1,500 members, and has been very successful in its work.

Michigan Yacht Club.—The club has a beautiful home of its own located on the American side of Belle Isle Park. The club house is always hospitably open to members and their guests, and an invitation to any of the club entertainments is well worth accepting.

Militia of Detroit—Is composed of seven companies of infantry, averaging about 75 members to each company, making two battalions, and with Company G, of Monroe, forming the 4th regiment of Michigan State troops. There is also a large band connected with the Detroit companies. Regimental headquarters are at 181 Jefferson avenue, the regiment's Colonel is in charge at Detroit, subject to the

Governor, who is commander-in-chief of the State troops. Part of the 4th regiment did duty at Fort Wayne in 1877. A battalion went to Bay City at the time of the riot there, and at different times they were under arms in Detroit armories during labor troubles. The companies are located as follows: A and F, cor. Jefferson avenue and Randolph street; D and H, 46 Congress street east; C, 224 Jefferson avenue; B and E, cor. Woodbridge and Shelby streets. The medical staff is composed of a surgeon and assistant, with hospital steward and details from each company. Company drills are held weekly at the different armories during the winter; skeleton battalion drills are held in one of the armories in warm weather; regular regimental and battalion drills are held out doors. The State troops conform in all respects, as far as possible, to U. S. Government rules and regulations, the uniform being identical, except the blouse for officers. The State troops are composed of five regiments, forming a brigade, headquarters of which are at Ypsilanti. The Adjutant General's office is at Lansing. Uniforms and accoutrements are furnished by the State Government.

Milk Inspector.—June 25, 1887, an Act entitled: "An Act to prevent the sale of impure, unwholesome, adulterated or swill milk in the State of Michigan, and to provide for inspectors," was approved by the Legislature of this State. Under this Act the present Milk Inspector was appointed and began his work under the supervision of the Health Board, February 9, 1888.

Mount Clemens.—One of the most delightful and probably the most famous of Detroit's many summer resorts is the City of Mt. Clemens, which is situated about 20 miles north of the city, on the Clinton river, a beautiful and picturesque stream that has its source among the numerous small lakes of Oakland county, winding its sinuous course eastward through miles upon miles of grassy meadows and luxuriant forests. Now swiftly bubbling over stretches of rapids, then again placidly pursuing its winding course through its shady banks until it reaches the Lake St. Clair. It presents at once to the tourist, the artist, the hunter, and the angler, a boon to be once seen and ne'er forgot. It is, as has been often remarked, "A thing of beauty and a joy forever."

The City of Mt. Clemens is one of the oldest towns in the State; the earliest settling of whites in its immediate vicinity dating back to 1731. Up to within ten years back its growth was comparatively slow, but since then it has more than doubled its population, which at present is about 6,000. It is the county seat of Macomb county, one of the best agricultural counties in the State. It has many beautiful buildings. Its schools, four in number, are second to none in the State, both as regards the personal acquirements and reputation of the teachers, and the solidity, beauty, safety and convenience of the structures. Seven religious denominations minister to the moral desires of the community, in as many churches, some of which are remarkable for their architectural beauty and design. A substantial and commodious opera house caters to the desires of theatre goers. The many beautiful homes, with their well-kept lawns, throughout the city, at once impress the tourist with the fact that the people of Mt. Clemens are cultivated, prosperous and happy. The city has ample telegraph and telephone

MOUNT CLEMENS. [COURT HOUSE.]

stem of electric
o things among
residence in a
ad and well
rives abound in
 Its hotel ac-
insurpassed by
the world. It
ubstantial and
s, which, with
s and private
c and comfort-
'or 3,000 people.
s is a delight-
ire seekers, its
esort is world-
n throngs of
g mortals seek
ving waters of
springs. They
1 stretchers, in
n and misery.
crutches, sans
fe and health,
ere exists such
in of health."
once de Leon
nd sought for
ith, instead of
very forests of
ive found it at
ne hence enjoy-
d health, after
derful waters.
rare medicinal
in any other
is a specific in
d nervous dis-

and handsome
appointments
valids and those
rely as a tonic,
ited in different

unication with
t, both by rail
nd Trunk Rail-
le accommoda-
while numerous
by way of Lake
St. Clair and up the Clinton, three miles to the city.

The Gratiot Road, a graveled and planked turnpike, extending from Detroit north to Mt. Clemens, makes a beautiful drive of two hours. We have every reason to believe that ere another year has rolled by Detroit will be connected with Mt. Clemens by a motor line on the Gratiot Road.

Mount Elliott Cemetery (Catholic).—Is located on Mt. Elliott avenue, near Champlain street, and is reached by Jefferson avenue and Fort Wayne electric cars. Additions have been made until it is now quite large; the grounds have been skillfully arranged and present a handsome appearance.

Mount Olivet Cemetery.—A new cemetery, half mile east of Norris, at Mt. Olivet Station, and can be reached by Grand Trunk Railway. This burying ground is used for Roman Catholics only.

Museums.—(See Art Museum.)

Musical Societies.—The following is a list of several of the principal musical societies and their location in Detroit:

CANSTATTER MAENNERCHOR, 129 Sherman street.

CONCORDIA SOCIETY, 265 Gratiot avenue.

DETROIT MUSICAL SOCIETY, 141 Woodward avenue.

DETROIT PHILHARMONIC CLUB, 87 Columbia street east.

DETROIT ZITHER CLUB, 1426 Jefferson avenue.

GERMAN SALESMEN, 87 and 89 Monroe avenue.

HARMONIE SOCIETY, cor. Champlain and Beaubien streets.

VETERAN SINGING SOCIETY, 175 Gratiot avenue.

Newspapers and Periodicals.—The following list gives the principal names of newspapers and periodicals in Detroit, with their offices, and subscription price per annum:

DAILIES.

Detroit Abendpost, $7, cor. Miami avenue and Wilcox street; German. Liberal Republican.

Detroit Free Press, $7, cor. Larned and Shelby streets. Democratic.

Detroit Journal (except Sundays), $3, cor. Larned and Shelby streets. Republican.

Detroit Tribune, $6, cor. Larned and Shelby streets. Republican.

Evening News, $5, 65 Shelby street. Independent.

Michigan Volksblatt (except Sundays), $6, 91 Gratiot avenue; German. Democratic.

WEEKLIES.

American Methodist, $1, 189 Woodward avenue.

American Tyler, $2, 42 Larned street west.

Angelus, $1, 62 Griswold street.

Der Arme Teufel, $2.50, 6 Champlain street; German. Radical.

Detroit Commercial Advertiser and Michigan Home Journal, $1.50, 11 Rowland street. Independent.

Detroit Courier, $1, 44, Larned street west.

Detroit Critic, 44 Larned street west.

Detroit Herald of Commerce, 18 Butterfield building.

Die Hauspost, 214 Randolph st.

Die Stimme der Wahrheit, 413 St. Aubin avenue; German, Catholic.

Echo, 60 cents, 65 Shelby street.

Familien Blaetter, $2, cor. Miami avenue and Wilcox street.

Fraternal Index, 75 cents, 55 and 57 Miami avenue.

Im Familienkreise, $1.25, 214 Randolph street.

Industrial Farm and Fireside, 19 Butterfield building.

Jugendpost, 75 cents, 214 Randolph street.

Kinderpost, 50 cents, 214 Randolph street.

Michigan Catholic, $2, 11 Rowland street.

Michigan Christian Advocate, $1.50, 189 Woodward avenue.

Michigan Farmer and State Journal of Agriculture, $1, 40 and 42 Larned street west.

Michigan Journal and Herald (semi-weekly), $2.50, 214 Randolph street.

Northside Gazette, $1.50, 1472 Woodward avenue.

Patriotic American, $2, 227 Jefferson avenue.

Plaindealer, $1, 11 Rowland street.

Prawda, 794 Twenty-fourth street. Polish, Independent.

Saturday Night, $1, 22 Clinton avenue.

Western Newspaper Union, $1, 22 Clinton avenue.

SEMI-MONTHLY.

Acker und Gartenbau Zeitung, $1.25, 214 Randolph street.

Medical Age, $1, foot of McDougall avenue.

MONTHLIES.

American Horse Monthly, Jefferson avenue, bet. Cass and First sts.

American Lancet, $2, foot of McDougall avenue.

Book-Keeper, 50 cents.

Bulletin of Pharmacy, $1, foot of McDougall avenue.

Collector, $1, Whitney Opera House building.

Detroit Dash, $1, 22 Clinton ave.

Detroit Globe, 50 cents, 700 Cass avenue.

Grace Hospital Compass, 11 Atwater street east.

Index Medicus, $10, foot of McDougall avenue.

Indicator, $2, 38 and 39 McGraw building.

International, $2, 54 State street.
International Masonic Review, 204 Eighth street.
Menschenfreund, $1, 248 Harvey avenue.
Michigan Herald, 50 cents, 15 Wilcox street.
Therapeutic Gazette, $2, foot of McDougall avenue.

Nurses.—Trained nurses may be obtained at any of the hospitals. There are also many private nurses who can be found by applying to any reputable physician.

Office Buildings.—There are many fine buildings in Detroit used exclusively for offices, the majority of which will be found on Griswold street, the Wall street of Detroit.

Orchard Lake—Is located on the D., G. H. & M. R. R., about 30 miles from Detroit, near Pontiac, and is one of the most beautiful of the handsome chain of lakes in that vicinity. The principal place of interest is the Orchard Lake Military Academy, which is under U. S. Government supervision.

Orion Lake—Is located on the Detroit & Bay City R. R., about 35 miles from Detroit, close to the village of Orion. It is a very popular place for excursions and campers, as it is full of small wooded islands. Orion Lake is one of the same chain of lakes as Orchard Lake.

Parks.—The following is a list of parks, with acreage:

Adelaide and Campau, 1.199 acres, Joseph Campau avenue, bet. Mullett street and Clinton avenue.
Belle Isle Park, see elsewhere, 750 acres.
Cass Park, 4.966 acres, Second avenue, bet. Ledyard and Bagg sts.
Clark Park, 24.731 acres, on Clark, Scotten and Dix avenues.
Clinton Park, 1.068 acres, bet. Gratiot and Clinton avenues, and Raynor and St. Antoine streets.
Crawford Park, 0.746 acres, cor. Fifth and High streets.
Elton Park, 0.740 acres, cor. Fifth and Orchard streets.
Grand Circus Park, 5.566 acres, Woodward avenue, from Park and Witherell to Adams avenue.
Macomb Park, 0.557 acres, Rose, Seventeenth and Eighteenth streets.
North Park, 0.448 acres, bet. Wilcox, Center and Randolph streets.
Stanton Park, 0.695 acres, Porter, Seventeenth and Eighteenth streets.
West Park, 0.740 acres, State, bet. Park and West Park place.
Opera House Lawn, 0.174 acres, Campus Martius.
Total park acreage, 741.630.

Parks and Boulevards, Commissioners of.—The commissioners of parks and boulevards were organized under an act of the Legislature, approved May 8, 1889 (succeeding the Board of Park and Board of Boulevard Commissioners, abolished by said act), and were given the control and management of the boulevard, and Belle Isle and other city parks. The commission consists of four resident electors, appointed by the common council on the nomination of the mayor; their appointment is for a term of four years, and they serve without compensation.

Pawnbrokers—Are compelled by law to give bonds for $1,000, and pay a license of $200 per year. They are also required to report daily to the police all articles received by them in pawn.

Picnic Grounds.—No city in the world can boast of more numerous or more pleasant places to picnic than Detroit has, within easy reach either by land or water, the cost of reaching them ranging from 10 cents to $1, according to distance. Following is a list of the more prominent places:

Belle Isle Park, Grosse Pointe, Sugar Island, St. Clair Flats, Grosse Isle, Put-in-Bay, Orion Lake, Des-Chree-Shos-Ka Orchard Lake, Walpole Island, Oak Grove, and many other places too numerous to mention.

Police.—The Metropolitan police force of the City of Detroit was organized by an act of the Legislature, approved February 28th, 1865, and entered upon its duties on the 15th day of May, 1865, under the direction of a board of commissioners, created by said act, who were vested with the entire control of the police force of the city. The commissioners receive no salary or compensation for their services. Since the 1st day of July, 1892, the board of Metropolitan police of the City of Detroit has been composed of four electors and freeholders of said city, appointed by the mayor. The members of the first board, organized under the new act, hold office for one, two, three and four years respectively. The police department comprises: Four captains, 24 sergeants, 29 roundsmen, 307 patrolmen, 21 doormen.

Besides the headquarters buildings, which contain the central station, there are ten other station houses, which are connected with headquarters, as follows:

Woodbridge street, near Woodward avenue.
Canfield avenue, near Chene street.
Fremont street, near Woodward avenue.
Gratiot avenue and Russell street.
Elmwood avenue, near Champlain street.
Trumbull avenue and Michigan avenue.
Twentieth street, near Michigan avenue.
River street, near Twenty-fourth street.
Scotten avenue, near Lafayette place.
Grand River avenue and Twelfth street.
Vinewood avenue, near Michigan avenue.
And a sub-station on Belle Isle.

Pontiac.—Is located on D., G. H. & M. R. R., about 25 miles from Detroit. It is one of the handsomest cities of its size in Michigan. Many Detroiters make their suburban home there during the summer. Orchard Lake Military Academy is easily reached from Pontiac. Pontiac Insane Asylum is located about two miles from the city.

Poor Commission.—The Legislature of 1879 abolished the office of Director of the Poor, and created the Board of Poor Commissioners instead. The board is composed of four members who shall serve without compensation. They have full charge of all matters appertaining to the care of the poor, and have power under the act to purchase and distribute provisions. clothing, fuel, medicines, etc., and may receive and disburse donations, and act in conjunction with any society or organization for charitable purposes. The board have also the disbursement of the County Temporary Relief Fund within the city. The Legislature of 1885 passed an act making the commissioners members of the Board of County Superintendents of the Poor, which gives the city a majority representation in the management of the County House and Asylum at Wayne. This act was declared constitutional by the supreme court, and the board is now acting under its provisions.

MUNICIPAL COURT BUILDING,
Cor. Clinton and Raynor Sts.

The commissioners are appointed by the common council on the nomination of the mayor, and their term of office is four years. An act of the Legislature, approved May 29, 1891, gives the board authority on the second Tuesday in June of each year to appoint three or more city physicians.

Population.—The growth in population is indicated in following table, from 1810 to 1892:

1810	770
1818	1,110
1820	1,442
1828	1,517
1830	2,222
1834	4,968
1840	9,102
1844	10,948
1850	21,019
1854	40,127
1860	45,619
1864	53,170
1870	79,599
1874	101,255
1880	116,342
1884	134,834
1890	205,877
1892	260.000

Post Office.—The business transacted at the Detroit postoffice outgrew the building at present occupied by the Government, and it was found necessary, about two years ago, to build a temporary annex, nearly as commodious as the original building, pending the completion of the new Federal building, in course of construction on Fort, Shelby and Wayne streets, and Lafayette ave. It will be the largest and handsomest building in Detroit when completed, costing upwards of $1,500,000. The postoffice at present is located corner Griswold and Larned streets, and the annex is located next to it on Larned street.

OFFICES AND LOCATION.—Postmaster, second floor, southwest corner building; office hours, 9 a. m. to 4 p. m. Assistant Postmaster, first floor, southwest corner building; office hours, 9 a. m. to 4 p. m. Cashier, first floor, southwest corner building; office hours, 9. a. m to 4 p. m. Superintendent City division, window in front of main building; office hours, 7.30 a. m. to 6 p. m. Superintendent of Mails, annex, entrance on Larned street, west of main building; office hours, 8 a. m. to 6 p. m. Money Order Department, annex, entrance on Larned street, west of main building; office hours, 9 a. m. to 5 p. m. Registered Letter Department, annex, entrance on Larned street, west of main building; office hours, 9 a. m. to 6 p. m. No business transacted in the Money Order and Registered Letter Departments on Sundays and holidays. Superintendent Second Class Matter, annex, entrance on Larned street, west of main building; office hours, 7.30 a. m. to 6 p. m. Second class matter delivered at west door, rear of annex. Special delivery division, annex, entrance on Larned street, west of main building. Stamp window, north end of corridor, open from 7.30 a. m. to 8 p. m.; Sundays, 12 m. to 1 p. m. General delivery, near center of corridor, open from 7.30 a. m. to 8 p. m.; Sundays, 12 m. to 1 p. m.

Postal Facilities.—STATIONS OF THE DETROIT POSTOFFICE.—Station A, No. 745 Woodward avenue, near corner of Alexandrine avenue. Station B, No. 807 Michigan avenue, near Humboldt avenue. Station C, No. 1212 Jefferson avenue, near Belt Line.

At these stations letters are registered, money orders and postal notes issued and paid, and postal supplies sold. Carriers report at and depart from these stations; in short, they furnish the public in their vicinity all the facilities obtainable at the general office, with this exception: no special delivery messengers are as yet assigned there.

Stations are open for the transaction of business from 7 a. m. to 6 p. m. week days, and on Sundays for the delivery of mail and the sale of stamps, etc., from 12 m. to 1 p.m.

SUB-STATIONS.—Hamtramck sub-station, corner Crane and Jefferson avenues

Gratiot avenue sub-station, at M. C. R. R. Belt Line station, Gratiot avenue, near Beaufait.

Pallister avenue sub-station, 1484 Woodward avenue.

Grand River avenue sub-station, first toll gate Grand River avenue.

West Detroit sub-station, Amos House, West Detroit.

River Road sub-station, on River Road, cor. Military avenue.

At these stations stamps, stamped envelopes, postal cards, special delivery stamps, etc., may be purchased, and letters registered. Mail may be left there on call, also, as the purpose of their establishment is principally for the convenience of persons residing outside the free delivery by carriers. No carriers make delivery from these stations, nor are money orders issued or cashed at them.

CARRIER DELIVERY. — Carriers are required to be prompt in making deliveries, to be courteous in their intercourse with the public, to deliver no mail matter except to the persons addressed or to their authorized agents (which includes servants, clerks, housekeepers, janitors and others, to whom such deliveries are recognized as valid by the addressees), to receive all prepaid letters, postal cards and small packages handed them for mailing while on their routes, and to collect the postage due on any mail matter delivered by them. Those assigned to duty on certain suburban districts are permitted to keep a limited number of postage stamps for sale to the public. Carriers are not permitted to deliver any mailable matter which has not passed through the postoffice, to exhibit, or to give information concerning any mail matter to persons other than those addressed, to engage in any private business (on their own account or for others) during their hours of official duty, to offer for sale or to deliver (except as mail matter) tickets or others articles, to issue New Year's or other addresses or cards, to solicit gifts of money or goods, to borrow money on their routes or contract debts which they are unable to pay, or deliver mail matter at unoccupied premises or on the street (except to persons known by them to be authorized to receive it). Carriers are not required to deliver packages the weight or bulk of which would tend to delay the delivery of letters or other mail matter. When such packages are received for delivery, notice is sent to the addressees to send or call for them at the postoffice.

On Sundays mail is delivered on call at the carriers' windows, both at the general office and stations, between 12 m. and 1 p. m. Collections are made by all carriers from the boxes as they deliver on their trips.

Collections are made by collectors with carts (in addition to those made by the carriers as they deliver) six times daily. Collectors leave the office at 6 a. m., 8.45 a. m., 12 m., and 2.45, 5.15, 6.15 and 9.15 p. m. in the business portion of the city.

Collections are also made at the principal hotels by collectors leaving the office at 5 a. m., 8.30 p. m. and 9.15 p. m.

The general collection by cart is made within the mile and a half radius from the City Hall, beginning at 10.45 a. m., of such boxes as are not included in the 12 m. collection, the carriers reaching the office at 1 p. m. This collection is repeated in the evening, the collectors leaving the office at 6.15 and returning at 8.45 p.m.

A collection is made every night in the week, excepting Saturday night, from all of the street letter boxes in the city, the collectors reaching the office at 5 a. m. Mail matter, deposited in any street letter box before 10.30 p. m., will therefore be taken up in time for dispatch by all early trains leaving after 5 a. m. and for first delivery by carriers in all parts of the city.

On Sundays one general collection of the boxes throughout the city is made, the collection commencing at 2.30 p. m., and reaching the office at 5.15 p. m. A collection from the principal hotels is made on Sundays at 9 a. m., 2.30 p. m. and 8 p. m.

Collections and deliveries on legal holidays are subject to such changes as the law prescribes or the postmaster may direct. Notice of changes are always announced in the daily papers.

SUGGESTIONS.—Expediting Carriers' Deliveries.—Carriers are required to deliver mail matter at stores, offices, or other business premises occupied by the persons addressed, in all cases where such deliveries are demanded; but persons occupying offices or stores on upper floors (especially in business buildings where elevators are not used) will greatly facilitate the work of the carriers by providing lock-boxes or other suitable means for the delivery of their mail matter on the first floor. This is, of course, not compulsory; but it is obvious that the general adoption of such a system will expedite the receipt of mail by all persons located on any carrier's route. For the same reason it is strongly recommended that boxes be affixed inside the doors of private residences, with openings through which carriers may deposit mail matter therein, and that at "apartment houses" boxes be provided for the purpose on the first floors. In all these cases a signal (by ringing door bell or otherwise) may be given by the carrier when delivery is made. When this plan is not adopted, however, the carrier, after ringing or knocking, is bound to wait a proper time for the appearance of some person to receive letters, etc., but must not delay the mail matter of other persons on his route by waiting for an unreasonable time. The schedule of carriers' deliveries is necessarily a *fixed* one, and the trips are so arranged as to secure the closest possible connection with mail arrivals (both inland and local) and with the collections from the street letter boxes. The routes are so served as to suit, as far as possible, the convenience of the majority of those residing or doing business thereon; but simultaneous delivery to all is not practicable, and those located on the more distant points of a route cannot reasonably expect deliveries as early as those made nearer to the starting point. On routes in business districts it sometimes happens that a few persons report that the first delivery reaches their premises before they are opened for business, but that they are unwilling to wait for the second delivery. In these cases the obvious and only remedy is to provide a box attached to the outer door, and connecting with an opening therein, through which mail may be delivered by carriers on the first trip.

SPECIAL DELIVERY.—The law establishing the special delivery system provides for the issue of a special stamp, of the face valuation of ten cents, which, when attached to a letter or package (in addition to the lawful postage thereon), will entitle such a letter or package to immediate delivery within the carrier limit of a free delivery office between the hours of 7 a. m. and 11 p. m., and within a radius of one mile from any other postoffice, by messengers, who, upon delivery, will procure receipts from the parties addressed, or some one authorized to receive them.

SUNDAY SPECIAL DELIVERY.— Up to 11 a. m.

GENERAL DELIVERY.—The general delivery is primarily designed for the delivery of the mail matter of transient residents and casual visitors; and permanent residents (except for special reasons) should not make use of it by having their correspondence so addressed; one reason for this suggestion being the possibility of the delivery of their letters, etc., to transient residents bearing the same names. All mail matter bearing no street or box address (and the proper addresses for which are not known and cannot be found in the directory), and all mail matter found undeliverable at its street address (and of which the correct address is not known and cannot be found in the directory) is placed in the general delivery to await call. If bearing the name and address of the sender, with a request to return within a specified time, it is, if uncalled for, returned at the expiration of that time; if no particular time is named in the request, or if it bears the name and address of the sender only, without request to return, it is returned at the expiration of thirty days if not previously called for. No mail matter bearing senders' names, addresses or requests is advertised.

RATES OF POSTAGE.—The rate of postage on mail matter of the first class (sealed or unsealed) is two cents for each ounce or fraction thereof, excepting postal cards, and excepting, also, letters for local delivery posted at a postoffice where no letter carriers are employed, in which case the rate is one cent per ounce or fraction thereof.

The rate of postage on mail matter of the second class, when posted by persons other than the publisher or news agents, is one cent for each four ounces or fraction thereof.

The rate of postage on mail matter of the third class is one cent for each two ounces or fraction thereof.

The rate of postage on mail matter of the fourth class is one cent per ounce or fraction thereof, except seeds, roots, bulbs, cuttings, scions and plants, the postage on which is one cent per two ounces or fraction thereof.

The rates of postage to the countries and colonies composing the Universal Postal Union (except Canada and Mexico) are as follows: Letters, per 15 grams (½ ounce), 5 cents; postal cards, each, 2 cents; newspapers and other printed matter, per 2 ounces, 1 cent; commercial papers, packets not in excess of 10 ounces, 5 cents; packets in excess of 10 ounces, for each 2 ounces or fraction thereof, 1 cent; samples of merchandise, packets not in excess of 4 ounces, 2 cents; packets in excess of 4 ounces, for each 2 ounces or fraction thereof, 1 cent; registration fee on letters or other articles, 10 cents.

MEXICO.—Matter mailed in the United States, addressed to Mexico, is subject to the same postage rates and conditions as it would be if it

GRISWOLD STREET—LOOKING SOUTH.

were addressed for delivery in the United States, except "commercial papers," which may be sent at the same rates and conditions as to other Postal Union countries, and except that articles of miscellaneous merchandise (fourth class matter) not sent as *bona fide* trade samples, are required to be sent by "parcels post," and that the following articles are absolutely excluded from the mails without regard to the amount of postage prepaid, or the manner in which they are wrapped, viz.:

All sealed packages, other than letters in their usual and ordinary form; all packages (including packages of second class matter, which weigh more than 4 pounds 6 ounces) except such as are sent by "parcels post;" liquids, pastes, confections, and fatty substances, publications which violate any copyright law of Mexico.

Single volumes of printed books, in unsealed packages, are transmissible to Mexico in the regular mails without limit as to weight.

Bona fide trade samples are transmissible to Mexico in the regular mails at the same rate and on same conditions as to other postal union countries.

CANADA.—Matter mailed in the United States, addressed to Canada, is subject to the same postage rates and conditions as it would be if it were addressed for delivery in the United States, except "commercial papers," which may be sent at same rates and conditions as to other postal union countries, and except that the following articles are absolutely excluded from the mails, without regard to the amount of postage prepaid or the manner in which they are wrapped, viz.:

All sealed packages other than letters in their usual and ordinary form; all packages (except single volumes of printed books and packages of second class matter), which weigh more than 4 pounds 6 ounces; publications which violate any copyright law of Canada.

REGISTERED LETTERS AND PARCELS.—Any article of the first, third or fourth class of mail matter may be registered at any postoffice in the United States.

The fee on registered matter, domestic or foreign, is 10 cents for each letter or parcel, to be affixed in stamps, in addition to the postage. Full prepayment of postage and fee is required. Two or more letters or parcels addressed to, or intended for, the same person, cannot be tied or otherwise fastened together and registered as one.

Every letter presented for registration must first be fully and legibly addressed and securely sealed by the sender, and all letters and other articles must also have the name and address of the sender endorsed thereon in writing or print before they can be registered.

Postmasters and their employees are forbidden to address a registered letter or package for the sender, to place contents therein, or to seal it, or to affix the stamps thereto; this, in all cases, must be done by the sender. Registered mail matter can only be delivered to the addressees in person or on their written order. All persons calling for registered matter should be prepared to furnish reasonable proof of their identity, as it is impossible otherwise, at large postoffices, to guard against fraud.

Safety is considered before celerity in the transmission of registered mail; and delays are sometimes necessary to secure prompt receipts at points of transfers, and due allowance must be made by those mailing such matter, and those to whom it is addressed, as registered mails cannot be handled with the same dispatch as ordinary mail matter.

A return receipt, signed by addressee, and showing delivery, is returned to the sender of each domestic registered letter or parcel, for which service there is no extra charge.

Letters and packages containing money or articles of value should be registered, and never be deposited for transmission by ordinary mails.

MONEY ORDERS.—When applying for money orders payable in the United States, the printed application forms should be used. The following are the fees payable thereon:

For sums not exceeding	$ 5			5 cts.
Over $ 5 and not	"	10		8 "
" 10	"	"	15	10 "
" 15	"	"	30	15 "
" 30	"	"	40	20 "
" 40	"	"	50	25 "
" 50	"	"	60	30 "
" 60	"	"	70	35 "
" 70	"	"	80	40 "
" 80	"	"	100	45 "

LIMIT OF AMOUNT OF SINGLE ORDERS.—A single money order may include any amount from one cent to one hundred dollars, inclusive; but must not contain a fractional part of a cent.

POSTAL NOTES.—LIMIT.— Postal Notes are issued for any sum from one cent to four dollars and ninety-nine cents ($4.99) inclusive, but not for any fractional part of a cent.

FEES.—The uniform fee for the issue of a postal note is three cents.

WHERE PURCHASED.—They can be purchased at the General Post-office, or any Branch Station.

WHERE PAYABLE.—Postal Notes are payable at any money order office in the United States. They are payable to bearer, and no identification is required.

INTERNATIONAL MONEY ORDERS, payable in the countries named below, are issued as follows:

Great Britain and Ireland,
Canada,
Germany,
France,
Italy,
Belgium,
Switzerland,
Sweden,
Norway,
Denmark,
Portugal,
Netherlands,
Luxemburg,
Austro-Hungary,
New So. Wales,
Queensland,
Windw'd Islands,
Ceylon,
Straits Settlem'ts (Singapore, Penang and Malacca),
Malta,
Beyrout,
Azores and Maderia Islands.

Victoria,
New Zealand,
South Australia,
West Australia,
Tasmania,
British India,
Japan,
Hawaii,
Jamaica,
Cape Colony,
Egypt,
Constantinople,
Hong Kong,
Bermuda,
Gibraltar,
Iceland,
Natal,
Leeward Islands,
Falkland Islands,
Gambia,
Mauritius,
St. Helena,
Trinidad,
Tangier,
Salonica,

FEES.—The following fees are charged for money orders issued on any of the countries named above:

On orders not exceeding	$10			10 cts.
Over $10 and not	"	20		20 "
" 20	"	"	30	30 "
" 30	"	"	40	40 "
" 40	"	"	50	50 "
" 50	"	"	60	60 "
" 60	"	"	70	70 "
" 70	"	"	80	80 "
" 80	"	"	90	90 "
" 90	"	"	100	$1.00 "

Distance in miles by the shortest post route and time in transit of mails between Detroit, Mich., and principal cities in the United States and Canada:

From Detroit to	Miles	Hrs.	Min.
Baltimore, Md.	655	25	..
Boston, Mass.	750	22	..
Chicago, Ill.	285	7	40
Cincinnati, Ohio	263	9	45
Denver, Col	1313	51	..
Hamilton, Ont.	186	5	35
London, Ont.	110	3	20
Minneapolis, Minn.	708	24	55
Montreal, Que.	558	18	45
New York, N. Y.	691	20	15
Omaha, Neb.	793	27	35
Philadelphia, Pa.	675	23	50
Pittsburgh, Pa.	321	12	35
Portland, Ore.	2753	111	55
St. Louis, Mo.	498	17	15
San Francisco, Cal.	2660	93	15
Toronto, Ont.	230	7	15
Washington, D. C.	695	26	..
Quebec, Que.	723	25	15

ABBREVIATION OF STATES AND TERRITORIES.—Mail matter is often missent and delayed by a wrong abbreviation of the State or Territory being given—Missouri abbreviated "Miss," would be sent to Mississippi; Indiana abbreviated "Ia." would be sent to Iowa, etc. The following is the approved abbreviation of names of all States and Territories:

Ala........Alabama.
Alaska....Alaska Territory.
Ariz......Arizona Territory.
Ark.......Arkansas.
Cal.......California.
Colo......Colorado.
Conn......Connecticut.
Del.......Delaware.
D. C......District of Columbia.
Fla.......Florida.
Ga........Georgia.
Idaho.....Idaho.
Ill.......Illinois.
Ind.......Indiana.
Ind. Ter...Indian Territory.
Iowa......Iowa.
Kans......Kansas.
Ky........Kentucky.
La........Louisiana.
Me........Maine.
Md........Maryland.
Mass......Massachusetts.
Mich......Michigan.
Minn......Minnesota.
Miss......Mississippi.
Mo........Missouri.
Mont......Montana.
Nebr......Nebraska.
Nev.......Nevada.
N. Dak....North Dakota.
N. H......New Hampshire.
N. J......New Jersey.
N. Mex....New Mexico Ter.
N. C......North Carolina.
N. Y......New York.
Ohio......Ohio.
Okla......Oklahoma.
Oregon....Oregon.
Pa........Pennsylvania.
R. I......Rhode Island.
S. C......South Carolina.
S. Dak....South Dakota.
Tenn......Tennessee.
Tex.......Texas.
Utah......Utah Territory.
Vt........Vermont.
Va........Virginia.
Wash......Washington.
W. Va.....West Virginia.
Wis.......Wisconsin.
Wyo.......Wyoming.

Presbyterian Churches. — The following list gives the names and location of those in Detroit:

BETHANY PRESBYTERIAN, Boulevard, near Jefferson avenue.

CAVALRY, Michigan avenue, opp. Maybury Grand avenue.

CENTRAL PRESBYTERIAN, cor. Bates and Farmer streets.

CHURCH OF THE COVENANT, cor. Russell and Napoleon streets.

FIRST PRESBYTERIAN, cor. Woodward avenue and Edmund place.

FORT STREET PRESBYTERIAN, cor. Fort and Third streets.

JEFFERSON AVENUE PRESBYTERIAN, Jefferson avenue, bet. Rivard and Russell streets.

MEMORIAL PRESBYTERIAN, n. e. cor. Clinton and Jos. Campau aves.

SECOND AVENUE PRESBYTERIAN, cor. Second avenue and Gilman st.

THOMPSON PRESBYTERIAN, cor. Woodward and Hendrie avenues.

TRUMBULL AVENUE PRESBYTERIAN, cor. Trumbull avenue and Brainard street.

WESTMINSTER PRESBYTERIAN, cor. Woodward avenue and Parsons street.

Prisons.—There is no State prison located in Detroit, but many prisoners are sent to the Detroit House of Correction by the State officials and also by other States and the U. S. Government. The House of Correction is located on Russell and Alfred streets, and is considered a model of its kind. (See House of Correction.)

Produce Exchange.—The Fruit and Produce dealers of Detroit, feeling the necessity of an organization, issued a call May 1st, 1893, at which time a meeting was held and a permanent organization formed, to be known as The Detroit Produce Exchange. The objects of the association are to concentrate action upon the general welfare of the trade, to collect and disseminate information, to improve business methods, to protest against unjust discrimination, exactions and damages of transportation, to demand integrity and fair dealing in financial operations, and to protect shippers and each other as far as possible against fraud, misrepresentation and injustice. The association at present is composed of 18 of the leading produce dealers in Detroit. The Exchange had not selected permanent quarters previous to issuing of this work. E. G. Newhall, corner Woodbridge and Griswold streets, is president.

Protestant Episcopal Churches.
—The following list gives the names and location of those in Detroit:

The residence of the Bishop is at 226 Fort street west.

ALL SAINTS' CHAPEL, Livernois avenue.

CHRIST CHURCH, south side Jefferson avenue, bet. Hastings and Rivard streets.

CHURCH OF OUR SAVIOUR, Leesville.

CHURCH OF THE MESSIAH, cor. Mt. Elliott avenue and Fort street.

EMANUEL CHURCH, west side Alexandrine avenue, bet. Woodward and Cass avenues.

GOOD SHEPHERD, Vinewood avenue, near Michigan avenue.

GRACE CHURCH, cor. Fort and Second streets.

MARINER'S CHURCH, cor. Woodward avenue and Woodbridge street.

ST. ANDREW'S CHURCH, cor. Fourth and Putnam avenues.

ST. BARNABAS' MISSION, Fourteenth avenue, near Grand River.

ST. GEORGE'S CHURCH, cor. Howard and Fourteenth avenue.

ST. JAMES' CHURCH, cor. Bagg and Seventh streets.

ST. JOHN'S CHURCH, cor. Woodward avenue and High street.

ST. JOSEPH'S MEMORIAL CHURCH, cor. Woodward and Medbury aves.

ST. LUKE'S MEMORIAL CHAPEL, at St. Luke's Hospital.

ST. MARY'S MISSION OF ST. JOHN'S CHURCH, cor. Benton and St. Antoine streets.

ST. MATTHEW'S (colored), cor. St. Antoine and Elizabeth streets.

ST. PAUL'S, cor. Congress and Shelby streets.

ST. PETER'S, cor. Trumbull avenue and Church street.

DETROIT CLUB.

St. Philip's Mission, east side of McDougall avenue, north of Gratiot avenue.

St. Stephen's Church, cor. Mullett street and St. Aubin avenue.

St. Thomas' Church, cor. Twenty-fifth street and Shady Lane.

Public Halls.—See Halls.

Public Library.—The Detroit public library was first opened to the public in the old Capitol building, (late High School building), on the 25th day of March, 1865, with 8,864 volumes. It was opened in the present building on the 22d day of January, 1877, with 33,604 volumes. The number of volumes on hand on the 1st day of January, 1893, was 115,661. The use of the library during the first year of its existence was 4,700 volumes. The use during the first year of the occupancy of the present building was 160,000, and during the last year it was about 600,000, or an average use of every book in the library upwards of five times during the year. This constant use wears out more than a thousand volumes every year. These are replaced, so far as possible, by new copies of the same books.

An excellent catalogue of the entire library is now in use. This is kept up to date as new books are added, so that it is possible to find out at once whether any given book is in the library or not.

The library is closely connected with the University Extension system, and special books are furnished and special facilities are given to students in these courses, as well as to persons connected with other reading circles. For this use of the library more room is demanded, and measures are now on foot looking to an enlargement of the building by erecting, on the front portion of the lot, a structure which shall be a credit to the city and serve its purposes for many years to come.

Public Works, Board of.—This board, established by request of the common council, by an amendment of the city charter, approved April 29, 1873, consists of three members, nominated by the mayor, and confirmed by the common council. The board is vested with control and supervision of the paving, repaving, cleaning, repairing, grading, working and improving of all streets, alleys, avenues and public grounds; the construction, altering and repairing of public wharves, docks, bridges, culverts, receiving basins, sewers and water courses; the laying of all side and cross walks; the construction of all drinking or ornamental fountains; the erection of all public buildings and works of the corporation, without the power, however, of changing the plans or specification of such work when once adopted. They report to the common council on the progress of any work, and all bills must be submitted to the said common council, who will then authorize the controller to draw his warrant therefor. The board took charge of all public works as above partially enumerated on the first day of January, 1874, and the offices of street commissioners, overseers of highways, city surveyor, the board of sewer commissioners, commissioners on plan of the city, and all other officers whose duties are now performed by the Board of Public Works, were abolished from and after the third Tuesday of January, 1874.

Railroads.—Trains arrive in and leave Detroit almost every minute, day and night. Fast through express trains leave Detroit several times daily for New York, Chicago, and other large cities, making close connections for all large cities in the United States. Railroads run direct from Detroit to all the large towns in the State of Michigan, and many cities in Indiana, Ohio and Canada.

CANADIAN PACIFIC.—From Union Depot, corner Fort and Third sts.

CHICAGO & GR'ND TRUNK —From foot of Brush street; depot of Detroit, Grand Haven & Milwaukee Ry.

DETROIT, BAY CITY & ALPENA.— From foot of Third street; depot of Michigan Central Ry.

DETROIT, GRAND HAVEN & MILWAUKEE.—From depot foot of Brush street.

DETROIT, LANSING & NORTHERN. —From Union Depot, Fort and Third streets.

DETROIT, MONROE & TOLEDO.— From foot of Brush street; depot of Detroit, Grand Haven & Milwaukee Ry.

DETROIT & BAY CITY.—From foot of Third street; depot of Michigan Central Ry.

FLINT & PERE MARQUETTE.— From Union Depot, corner Fort and Third streets.

GRAND TRUNK.—From foot of Brush street; depot of Detroit, Grand Haven & Milwaukee Ry.

LAKE SHORE & MICHIGAN SOUTHERN.—From foot of Brush street; depot of Detroit, Grand Haven & Milwaukee Ry.

MICHIGAN CENTRAL—From depot foot of Third street.

WABASH RAILROAD.—From Union Depot, corner Fort and Third sts.

Real Estate Board.—See Detroit Real Estate Board.

Register of Deeds.—Office located on first floor, City Hall.

Riding Club.—The Detroit Riding Club was organized during the season of 1891-2, at the suggestion of one of the oldest members of the New York Riding Club. The Club secured the Princess Rink, which was one of the largest buildings of its kind in the city, and fitted up stables for 41 horses, and one of the largest rings in the country, also very convenient club rooms, with dressing rooms and lockers for both ladies and gentlemen. The Club has proven very popular with the best people in the city. Many of our most prominent people take advantage of it as valuable education for the young people and children in the art of horseback riding. The Club has a membership of 150, and the opening of the season, October 1st. they expect to inaugurate a good many new features, in the way of classes in cavalry tactics, tandem-driving, and bare-back riding. The Club were so successful with their horse show, which was the first of the kind ever given in Detroit that they have in preparation another for next season on a very much larger scale. The season is from October 1st to May 1st, during which time the school is open for classes from 9 to 12 A. M., and 2 to 4 P. M., and evenings from 7:30 to 10, excepting Wednesday and Saturday, which are reserved for regular Club riding. A great many of our business and professional men, who are members, ride in the ring during the winter and unpleasant weather, from 4 to 6 P. M. It is the best exercise one can take. The membership fee is $50, and dues $30 per year.

Rogues' Gallery.—The Rogues' Gallery has been thoroughly revised; a large number of "deads" and duplicates weeded out, and the whole, including both home and foreign photographs, indexed. Number of photographs, home, 1694; number of photographs, foreign, 825.

The adoption of the American Bertillon System for measuring prisoners—a system unerring in the positive identification of a person once subjected to its test, also, the photographing of criminals, and others who are taken into custody and whose faces find a place in the Rogues' Gallery—previously done outside of the department—is now performed within the walls of Headquarters Building.

By this method much time and annoyance is saved, and the subjects so photographed are less likely to become obstreperous, and submit more readily to the process than when compelled to be taken through the streets, in the custody of an officer, to a photograph gallery as heretofore.

This part of the department service is under the immediate direction of the chief clerk in the Superintendent's office, an experienced and practical photographer, and the introduction of photography into the building is one of the new features which has from the beginning, been a success and not an experiment.

With increased facilities for the work in hand, the cost to the department of producing its own pictures of criminals can be reduced to the minimum, and results reached second to none obtained by other departments of police throughout the country, of which there are a number operating a like system.

Roman Catholic Churches.—The following list gives the names and location of those in Detroit. The Bishop's residence is at 31 Washington avenue.

Church of Our Lady of Help, corner Congress street and Elmwood avenue.

Church of Our Lady of the Rosary, Harper avenue, between Woodward avenue and John R street.

Church of Our Lady of Sorrows (Belgian), Catherine street, near Gratiot ave.

Church of the Most Holy Redeemer, corner Dix and Junction avenues.

Church of St. Francis, corner Buchanan street and Campbell avenue.

Church of SS. Peter and Paul, corner Adelaide and John R streets.

Church of SS. Peter and Paul, corner Jefferson ave. and St. Antoine street.

Most Holy Trinity, corner Porter and Sixth streets.

Sacred Heart (German), corner Rivard and Eliot streets.

St. Albert's (Polish and Slavic), corner St. Aubin and Canfield aves.

St. Aloysius', Washington avenue near State street.

St. Anne's (French), corner Howard and Nineteenth streets.

St. Anthony's, corner Gratiot and Field avenues.

St. Bonaventure's, corner Mt. Elliot and St. Paul avenues.

St. Boniface (German), corner Thirteenth and High streets.

St. Casimir's (Polish), corner Twenty-third and Myrtle streets.

St. Charles', Townsend avenue, between Agnes and St. Paul avenues.

St. Elizabeth's, corner McDougall and Canfield avenues.

St. Joachim's (French), corner Du Bois and Fort streets.

St. Josaphat's (Polish), n. s. Canfield avenue. near St. Antoine street.

St. Joseph's (German), corner Orleans and Jay streets.

St. Leo's, corner Grand River ave. and Fifteenth street.

St. Mary's (German), corner Monroe avenue and St. Antoine street.

St. Vincent de Paul, Fourteenth avenue, between Dalzelle and Marentette streets.

St. Wenceslaus, (Bohemian), Leland street, between Beaubien and St. Antoine streets.

Rooms.—Rooms can be obtained in almost any part of the city; prices ranging from 10 cents to elegant private residences, where room rent requires a large income.

Rowing.—There are numerous clubs formed for developimg this healthy sport; nearly all having club houses or headquarters near Belle Isle bridge approach, and hundreds of amateurs, of both sexes, can be seen any bright day on the river, and the island lakes and canals.

Safe Deposit Vaults.—Nearly all the banks in Detroit are provided with these vaults, which are for individual use. Those who rent a box are provided with a key, same as a postoffice box; no two keys are alike.

St. Clair Flats.—See Flats.

St. Mary's Hospital—Is located on St. Antoine street, bet. Mullett and Clinton avenue, opp. Clinton park, and is a very commodious and substantial structure. It is under the charge of the Sisters of Charity.

Seeds.—Detroit furnishes a large territory with seeds, one of the largest seed companies in the world being located here, namely, D. M. Ferry & Co., cor. Monroe avenue and Brush street. The immense establishment is considered one of the sights of the city, and well repays a visit of inspection.

Servants—Can be obtained by applying at any of the numerous intelligence offices, or by inserting an advertisement in one of the daily papers; wages range from $2 per week and board up, according to ability.

Shaary Zedeck Cemetery—Located on north side of Pallister avenue, between Dubois and Chene streets, and is owned by the Society of the Synagogue and Shaary Zedeck.

Sheriff's Office.—The office of the Sheriff of Wayne county is in the city hall, on the third floor. Business hours, from 9 a. m. to 4 p. m.

Sight-Seeing.—It depends, to a large extent, what class of sights the visitor wishes to see, as tastes differ in this as in other things. Probably the principal places of interest for most visitors in summer will be the river, Belle Isle Park, St. Clair Flats, Des-Chree-Shos-Ka, and other river pleasure resorts; a walk, drive, or street car ride through the main avenues will reveal many beautiful churches, schools, residences, etc.; a good view of the city and river can be obtained from the city hall tower. There are also the following places which would be worth visiting: Public Library, Art Museum, Waterworks, Grand Circus Park, House of Correction, Boulevard, Soldiers' and Sailors' Monument, Bagley Fountain, Fort Wayne, and many other places of interest. For those who enjoy machinery, etc., there is the great power-houses of the Fort Wayne and Belle Isle Electric Street Railroad and Citizens' Street Railway Co., and along the river front will be found many large factories, some of them the largest of their kind in the world. Those who prefer the large retail stores will find them on Woodward avenue and vicinity. The wholesale houses will be found mostly on lower Jefferson avenue and vicinity. An interesting place for business men to visit is Griswold street, the Wall

BELLE ISLE PARK BRIDGE—APPROACH FROM JEFFERSON AVENUE

street of Detroit, especially at the time of closing the clearing house, as that is usually the liveliest part of the day. (See Clearing House; see also Amusements.)

Signal Service.—The Detroit station is located on the top of the Hammond Building, cor. Griswold and Fort streets. A superstructure is fitted up for the use of the observer in charge and his assistants. Reports are received by telegraph from about 150 stations. Observations are taken and sent to these stations. Cautionary signals are displayed whenever a storm is threatened. This is also headquarters for the Michigan Weather Service.

Skating—Is a very popular sport in Detroit. The city has erected a large casino or pavilion on the edge of one of the artificial lakes at Belle Isle Park for the exclusive use of skaters in the winter. There are separate rooms for each sex, and thousands go there every year during the season. Admission is free. There are also many private rinks in the city.

Soldiers' and Sailors' Monument.—Is located opposite the city hall, and contains some very fine bronze statues.

Steamboats—Of all sizes, from the diminutive steam launch to the powerful and commodious lake vessels, can be seen at all times of the day or night on the river. The Detroit and Cleveland steamers are the largest and most elegantly furnished passenger boats on the lakes, and the Detroit, Belle Isle and Windsor Ferry Co.'s boats are the finest of their class. All vessels passing to or from Chicago and the east must go and come by way of the Detroit river, and at times the scene is a very interesting one.

Storage Companies.—There are several large buildings in Detroit devoted to storage purposes, where parties, leaving town or for other reasons, can leave anything from a hand satchel to a houseful of furniture. Some of the companies will advance money on goods stored with them. Following is a list of the principal storage companies, with their location:

Central Storage Co., 16 Gratiot avenue.
Fidelity Storage Co., 27 and 29 Woodward avenue.
Moreton Truck and Storage Co. (Ltd.), 25 to 29 Griswold street.
Riverside Storage Co. (Ltd.), 45 to 55 Woodbridge street east.
Security Storage Co., rear 179 John R. street.

Stoves.—Detroit is famous for its great stove works, there being four of the largest stove manufactories in the world located here. Stoves of any description, from the small plain box stove to the massive and artistic base burner, or from the smallest plain cook-stove to the immense modern range, are manufactured in these factories. Their names are The Michigan Stove Co., The Detroit Stove Works, The Peninsular Stove Co., and The Art Stove Co.

Street Railway Routes.—DETROIT CITIZENS' STREET RAILWAY. —Jefferson avenue—From the Michigan Central depot at intersection of Jefferson avenue and Third street, up Jefferson avenue to water works —4½ miles.

Woodward avenue—On Woodward avenue, from the river to the railroad tracks—3 1-6 miles.

Michigan avenue — From the river on Woodward avenue to Michigan avenue, on Michigan to city limits—4 1-10 miles.

Gratiot avenue—From the river on Woodward avenue to Monroe, to Randolph, to Gratiot, on Gratiot avenue to city limits—4 miles.

Grand River avenue—From the river on Woodward avenue to Grand River, to Boulevard—4 1-10 miles.

Myrtle street—From the river on Woodward avenue to Grand River, to Myrtle street, to Vinewood avenue—3⅓ miles.

Crawford street—From the river on Woodward avenue to Grand River, to Crawford street, to railroad tracks—3⅓ miles.

Cass and Third avenues—From intersection of Jefferson avenue and Third street on Third to Larned, to Griswold, to State, to Cass, to Ledyard, to Third avenue, to Holden avenue to railroad tracks—3¾ miles.

Trumbull avenue—From river on Woodward to Michigan, to Trumbull, to railroad tracks, and from Michigan avenue to Baker on Trumbull—3⅔ miles.

Congress & Baker—From intersection of Woodward avenue and Congress street on Congress to Seventh, to Baker, to Twenty-fourth street—4 miles.

Brush & Russell—From river on Woodward avenue to Monroe, to Gratiot to Brush, to Rowena, to Antoine, to Farnsworth, to Russell, to Grand Trunk Railroad tracks, and from Russell on Ferry to Lake Shore and Michigan Southern Railroad tracks—4 miles.

Chene street—From foot of Jos. Campau avenue to Atwater street, to Chene street, on Chene street to railroad tracks—5 miles.

Mack avenue—From intersection of Gratiot and Mack avenues on Mack avenue to Baldwin avenue—1 1-10 miles.

Loop Line—From intersection of Woodward avenue and Congress street on Congress street to Brush, to Fort, to Mt. Elliott, to Congress, on Congress back to Woodward avenue, and on Mt. Elliott from Fort street to Jefferson avenue—3 miles.

Third street—From intersection of Grand River avenue and Third street on Third street to Jefferson avenue—⅞ mile.

Brush street depot—From intersection of Congress street and Woodward avenue on Congress to Randolph, to Atwater, to D., G. H. & M. and G. T. R. R. depots, and from intersection of Woodward avenue and Atwater street on Atwater to above named depots—⅓ mile.

Detroit Suburban Railway.—Grosse Pointe Line—From water works on Jefferson avenue to Grosse Point—4½ miles.

Mack road—From intersection of Baldwin and Mack avenues on Mack to Clark, to Jefferson avenue, Grosse Pointe—6 miles.

Norris road—From city limits and Chene street on Chene to Carpenter road, to Conant road, to Davidson boulevard, to village of Norris, to Center Line road—5¼ miles.

Highland Park—From railroad tracks on Woodward avenue to Medbury road—3¾ miles.

Fort Wayne & Belle Isle Railway.—From near Baldwin avenue, down Champlain street to Elmwood avenue, along Elmwood avenue to Monroe avenue, down Monroe avenue to Randolph street, down Randolph street to Cadillac square, thence to Woodward avenue and along Fort street to Clark avenue, down Clark avenue to River street, along River street to River Rouge, where connection is made with the Wyandotte & Detroit River Railway; also on Champlain street from Elmwood avenue to Randolph street, thence on Bates street to Cadillac square and along Cadillac square to Woodward avenue and Fort street, making a loop line between Woodward and Elmwood avenues. Also on Dearborn road from River street to Fort street, and thence on Fort street to Clark avenue, and on Helen avenue from Champlain street to Belle Isle bridge approach.

The distance on the main line from Baldwin avenue to the River Rouge is 11 miles.

Streets, Directory of.—Woodward avenue divides the city exactly into its eastern and western halves, and all streets crossing it are called east or west as the case may be. For instance, High street east and High street west each has its own set of numbers, commencing at Woodward ave. Other streets running east or west commence their numbering from the end nearest to Woodward ave., while all streets running north and south commence numbering from the south (or river) end.

A, from 839 Vinewood ave., west to Hubbard ave.

A. T. Fischer ave., from Jefferson ave., north to Sherman st.

Abbott, from 125 Michigan ave., west to 12th st.

Aberle, from Russell, east to Dequindre.

Adair, from Detroit river, north to 1015 Jefferson ave.

Adams ave. east, from 274 Woodward ave., east to Hastings st.

Adams ave. west, from 275 Woodward ave., west to Grand River ave.

Adel, from Center Line ave., north to Strong.

Adelaide, from 428 Woodward av., east to Gratiot ave.

Agnes ave., from Boulevard, east to Crane.

Albert, from Clark ave., west to McKinstry.

Albert, from Wesson ave., west to D., L. & N. R. R.

Albert ave., from Grand River ave., east to Tefft.

Albert Place, from Dequindre, east to St. Aubin ave.

Alexandrine ave. east, from 746 Woodward ave., east to Gratiot.

Alexandrine ave. west, from 747 Woodward avenue, west to Grand River.

Alfred, from 456 Woodward ave., east to Dubois.

Alfred ave., from Fort st. west, north to Toledo ave.

Alger, from Russell, east to D., G. H. & M. R. R., beyond Boulevard.

Alger ave., from Woodward ave., east to Oakland, north of Boulevard.

Alger Place, Oakland ave., east to Cameron ave., north of Boulevard.

Anderson ave., from River Road north to St. Clair.

Anthon, from Junction ave., west to Military ave.

Antietam, from rear of 362 Gratiot ave., east to Elmwood ave.

Antoinette, from Woodward ave., west to Eighteenth.

Arlington Place, from 1145 Woodward ave., west to Cass.

Arndt, from 740 Gratiot ave., east to Meldrum.

Arthur, from Chene st., east.

Artillery ave., from River road, north to Dix.

Ash, from 505 Grand River ave., west to Vinewood ave.

Atwater st. east, from 24 Woodward ave., east to Adair.

Atwater st. west, from 23 Woodward ave., west to Shelby.

Aurelia, from 1049 Twelfth st., west to Wabash ave.

Avery ave., from 665 Grand River ave., north to Boulevard.

B, from 817 Vinewood, west to Detroit & Bay City Ry.

STR—STR

Bacon (Delray), from Springwells ave., west to West End ave.
Bagg, from 457 Woodward ave., west to Sixteenth.
Bagley ave., from Grand Circus Park, southwest to Cass.
Baker, from 182 Sixth, west to Scotten ave.
Baldwin ave., from 1525 Jefferson ave., north to Gratiot ave.
Baltimore avenue east, from 1462 Woodward ave., east to Boulevard.
Barclay Place, from 19 Wilcox, northwest to John R st.
Bates st., from Detroit river, northeast to Randolph st.
Battery ave., from Dragoon ave., west to city limits.
Bayonette ave., from Dragoon ave., west to city limits.
Beacon, from 292 Brush, east to rear 221 Gratiot ave.
Beard, from Fort st. west, north to Toledo ave.
Beaubien, from 115 Atwater st. east, north to city limits,
Beaufait ave., from 1225 Jefferson ave., north to Gratiot ave.
Beaver, from 27th, west first south of Hancock ave.
Beech, from 274 First, west to Seventh.
Bellair, from 708 Riopelle, east to Collins.
Belle Isle ave, from Parker north.
Bellevue ave., from 1271 Jefferson ave., north to city limits.
Belmont ave., from Woodward ave., east to Oakland ave., north of Boulevard.
Benton, from 600 Brush, east to Russell.
Berlin, from 704 Gratiot ave., east to Mt. Elliott ave.
Bethune ave., from Woodward ave., west to Second ave., north of Boulevard.
Biddle, from 27th west, first north of Merrick ave-
Bismarck ave., from Chene, east to M. C. R. R. Belt Line.

Blaine ave., from Woodward ave., west to Crawford, north of Boulevard.
Bohemian, from 1228 Second ave., east to Cass ave.
Boone, from McDougall ave., east to Moran st.
Boulevard east, from 1510 Woodward ave, east and south to Jefferson ave. and Belle Isle Bridge.
Boulevard west, from 1513 Woodward ave., west and south to Detroit river.
Brady, from 654 Woodward ave., east to Russell.
Brainard, from 627 Cass, west to Trumbull.
Brandon ave., from Scotten ave., west to Junction ave.
Bratshaw ave., from Third ave., west to Fourth ave.
Breckenridge, from 919 Grand River ave., west to Humboldt ave.
Brevoort Place, from rear of 105 Eighteenth, west to Twenty-second.
Brewster, from 524 Brush, east to Gratiot.
Brigham, from 835 Third ave., west to Grand River.
Bringard ave., from Crane ave., east.
Bristol Place, from 231 Twenty-first, west to Twenty-second.
Brush, from 81 Atwater st., north to city limits.
Bryant, from 1135 Twelfth, west to Wabash.
Buchanan, from 833 Grand River ave., west to Junction ave.
Burdeno ave. (Delray), from Springwells ave., west to Dearborn road.
Burlage Place, from Waterloo, north to Hendricks.
Bushey, from Michigan ave., south to Julia.
Butternut, from 463 Seventh, west to Twenty-fourth.
C, from 779 Vinewood ave., west to Hubbard ave.

CASINO—BELLE ISLE PARK.

Cadet ave., from Cavalry ave., west to Waterman ave.
Cadillac ave., from Jefferson ave., opposite Waterworks, north to Leesville.
Cadillac Square, from 138 Woodward ave., east to Randolph.
Calhoun, from 590 Brush, east to Grandy ave.
Cameron ave., from Pallister ave., north to Mersino.
Campau, from 1219 River, north to Wolff.
Campbell ave., from River, north to city limits.
Campus Martius, at junction of Michigan, Woodward and Monroe aves.
Canfield ave. east, from 816 Woodward ave., east to city limits.
Canfield ave. west, from 821 Woodward ave., west to Grand River.
Caniff ave., from Woodward ave., east to Oakland.
Caniff road, from Woodward ave., west to city limits.
Canton, from 1345 Jefferson ave., north to Harper.
Carbon, from Day ave., east to Dearborn road.
Cardoni, from Holbrook road, south.
Caroline, from 967 Twelfth, west to Wabash ave.
Carter, from Regular ave., north to Dix ave.
Carter Place. from Wilson ave., west to city limits.
Caspar, from Toledo ave., north.
Cass, from 117 Woodbridge, north to Grand River ave.
Cass ave., from 100 Grand River ave., north to Boulevard.
Catherine, from 199 Gratiot ave., east to Elmwood ave.
Cavalry ave., from 1541 Fort st. west, north to Toledo ave.
Celeron, from Junction ave., west to Campbell ave.
Celia, from 995 Twelfth, west to Wabash.

Center, from 255 Randolph st., northwest to John R.
Center Line ave., from junction of Mt. Elliott and Harper aves., northeast, beyond city limits.
Central ave., from Toledo avenue, north to Michigan avenue.
Chamberlain, from L. S. & M. S. Ry., west.
Champlain, from 176 Randolph, east to Van Dyke.
Chandler, from Junction ave., west to Campbell ave.
Chandler ave., from Woodward ave., east to Oakland.
Charles, from 147 Crawford, west to Eighth.
Charlevoix, from 524 Chene, east to Elmwood.
Charlotte ave., from 507 Woodward ave., west to Grand River.
Chase, from 58 Russell, east to Riopelle.
Chene, from 633 Atwater st. east, north to city limits.
Cherry, from 213 Grand River, west to Twelfth.
Chestnut, from 278 Russell, east to Elmwood.
Chipman, from rear of 267 Eighteenth, west to Nineteenth.
Chope Place, from Twenty-fifth, at McGraw ave., northeast to Campbell ave.
Church, from 441 Michigan ave., west to Twelfth.
Cicotte ave., from Southern ave., north to Michigan ave.
Clairmount Place, from Woodward ave., west to Wilson ave.
Clark ave., from River road, north to Michigan.
Cleveland, from 454 St. Aubin, east to Burlage place.
Cleveland ave., from Woodward ave., west to Crawford, and from Cameron ave. east to Russell.
Cleveland Place, from 538 Crawford, east to Fourth ave.
Clifford, from 235 Woodward ave.,

west and north to junction of Ledyard and Cass.
Clinton, from A. T. Fisher ave., east to Crane ave.
Clinton avenue, from junction of Brush and Gratiot, east to Elmwood.
Cobb, from junction of Boulevard and McGraw ave., northwest to Scotten ave.
Coe, from Bellevue ave., east to Belle Isle ave.
Colby, from Russell, east to Dequindre.
Collins, from 949 Gratiot, north to Griffin.
Columbia east, from 312 Woodward, east to Rivard.
Columbia west, from 313 Woodward, west to Cass ave.
Columbus, from Detroit & Bay City Ry., west to Scotten ave.
Columbus ave., from River, north to Fort.
Commonwealth ave., from 620 Grand River, north to Holden ave.
Concord ave., from the river, north to Harper ave.
Congress east, from 110 Woodward, east to Baldwin.
Congress west, from 109 Woodward, west to Seventh.
Copland ave. (Delray), from River road, north to M. C. R. R., west of Dearborn road.
Cottrell ave. (Delray), from Kerchval, west to Anderson ave.
Craig, from Trombly, north to Milwaukee ave.
Crane ave., from the river, north to Gratiot ave.
Craven ave., from Cass ave., west to Crawford.
Crawford, from 382 Grand River ave., north to city limits.
Crawford ave., from Fort st. west, north to Regular ave.
Cross, from 66 John R., east to Randolph.
Crossley ave. (Delray), from River road, opp. Exposition Grounds, north to St. Clair.
Crystal, from Trombly ave., north to Milwaukee ave.
Custer ave., from Woodward ave., east to Hastings.
Cutler ave., from McClellan ave., east.
D, from Vinewood ave., west to Hubbard ave.
Dalzelle, from 311 Twelfth, west to Twenty-fourth.
Dane, from Collins.
Danforth, from Lumpkin avenue, east to Jos. Campau ave.
Davenport, from 637 Woodward ave., west to Cass ave.
Davis Place, from Forest ave., north to Theodore.
Dearborn road (Delray), from River road, northwest.
Dennis, from Livernois ave., west to Clippert ave.
Denton ave., from St. Aubin ave., east.
Dequindre, from Detroit river, north to city limits.
Detroit, from G. T. Ry., north.
Dettloff Court, between Hancock and Warren aves, first east of Moran.
Devereaux, from Twenty-eighth, west to Campbell ave.
Devogelaer, from McClellan ave., east.
Dey, from Rogueville road, north.
Division, from 480 Brush, east to St. Aubin ave.
Dix ave., from rear 305 Twenty-second, west to River Rouge.
Dorchester, from McClellan ave, east.
Dragoon ave., from River road, north to Toledo ave.
Driggs, from Junction ave., west to Campbell ave.
Dry Dock, from Minnie, west to Pleasant ave.
Dubois, from 558 Atwater st. east, north to Boulevard.
Duffield 371 Woodward ave., west to Cass ave.
Dumontier ave., from Crane ave., east.

Dunn, from Junction ave., parallel with M. C. R. R., west to Wesson ave.
E, from 506 Twenty-third, west to Hubbard ave.
Edmund Place, from opposite 493 Woodward ave., east to Brush.
Edward, from Cicotte ave., west, first south of Michigan ave.
Eighteenth. from 746 Fort st. west, north to city limits.
Eighteenth-and-a-half, from Detroit river, north to 797 Fort st. west.
Eighth, from 346 River, north to Lysander.
Eliot. from 600 Woodward ave., east to Riopelle.
Elizabeth east, from 292 Woodward, east to rear of 315 Gratiot.
Elizabeth west, from 391 Woodward, west to Grand River ave.
Ellery, from 385 Waterloo, north to Trombly.
Ellery Place, from 1011 Forest east north to Hancock.
Elm. from 485 Seventh, west to Wabash.
Elmwood ave., from 983 Jefferson ave., north to Willis ave.
Elsa, from McClellan ave. east, north of Mack ave.
Elwood, from Campbell ave., west to D. L. & N. R. R.
Emerson, east from Central ave., third south of Michigan ave.
Endicott ave., from 1416 Woodward ave., east to John R.
Englewood ave., from Woodward ave. east to Oakland ave.
Eric (Delray), from Kercheval, west to Anderson ave.
Erskine, from 564 Woodward ave., east to Brush.
Euclid ave., from Woodward ave., west to Crawford.
Exposition ave. (Delray). from River road, opposite exposition entrance, north to St. Clair.
'F'. from Vinewood ave., west to Hubbard ave.

Fairview ave., from Woodward ave., west.
Farmer, from 155 Randolph, northwest to Wilcox.
Farnsworth, from 1040 Woodward ave., east to Boulevard.
Farrand, from McClellan ave., east.
Farrand ave., from Woodward ave., east.
Farrar, from junction of Randolph and Bates, northwest to Wilcox.
Ferdinand ave., from 1420 River, north to Toledo ave.
Ferry ave., from 1170 Woodward, east to Boulevard.
Field, from Livernois ave., west.
Field, from Fort st. west, north to L. S. & M. S. Ry.
Field ave., from 1443 Jefferson ave., north to city limits.
Fifteenth, from 683 Fort st. west, north to boulevard.
Fifth, from 254 River, north to Piquette.
Fifth ave., from Woodward ave., west to Twelfth.
First, from Detroit river, north to 151 Grand River.
Fletcher, from 1643 Michigan, west to railroad.
Florence, from Harper ave., north to Piquette ave.
Flower, bet. Forest and Hancock aves east, Grandy ave. and Chene st.
Fordyce ave., from Lincoln, north to Holbrook ave., bet. Dequindre and St. Aubin ave.
Forest ave. east, from 896 Woodward, east to city limits.
Forest ave. west, from 881 Woodward, west to Vinewood.
Forsyth ave., from Holden ave., north to Boulevard
Fort st. east, from 146 Randolph, east to Helen ave.
Fort st. west, from 131 Woodward ave., west to city limits.
Foundry, from 496 Baker, north to Michigan ave.

STR—STR

Fourteenth ave., from 664 Fort st. west, north to city limits.
Fourth, from 250 River, north to Grand River ave.
Fourth ave., from 316 Grand River ave., north to city limits.
Fourth ave., from Woodward ave., west to Crawford ave.
Fox, from 88 Frank, north to Alexandrine ave. west.
Francis, from Baker, at M. C. R. R., northwest to Eighteenth.
Frank, from 663 Fourth ave., west to Seventh.
Franklin, from 40 Randolph, east to Leib.
Frederick, from 1060 Woodward ave., east to city limits.
Front, from 9 First, west to Third.
G. A. R., from Hammond ave., west to Welch ave.
Gallagher Place, from rear 819 Fourth ave., west to Crawford.
Garfield ave., from 830 Woodward ave., east to Helen ave.
Garfield Place, from 506 Lafayette ave., north to Howard.
Genesee, east of Mt. Elliott ave.
Gilbert, from Southern ave., north to Linzee ave.
Gilbert ave., from Hubbard ave., west to Scotten ave.
Gilbert Place, from Schmittdiel ave., west to limits.
Gilman, from 313 Cass, west to Second ave.
Gladstone, from Twenty-seventh, west to Vinewood.
Gladstone ave., from Woodward ave., west to Crawford ave.
Glen ave., from Oakland ave., east to Cameron.
Glendale ave., from Woodward, west to Hamilton boulevard.
Glynn Court, from Woodward, west to Crawford.
Godfroy, north from Center Line ave.
Gold, from 949 Third ave., west to Fourth ave.

Goldner ave., from G. T. Ry., north to Michigan ave.
Goldsmith ave., west from Waterman ave.
Goodson, from Lumpkin ave., east to Chene.
Govin, from Fort st. west, north to Porter.
Grand River ave., from 205 Woodward ave., northwest to city limits.
Grandy ave., from 804 Gratiot ave., north to Milwaukee ave.
Grant, from 741 Twelfth, west to Wabash ave.
Grant Court, from 254 Warren ave. west, north to Putnam ave.
Granville Place, from 773 Thirteenth, west to Wabash.
Gratiot avenue, from 164 Woodward ave., northeast beyond city limits.
Grayling, from Lumpkin ave., east to Chene.
Green ave., from 358 Holden ave., northeast to boulevard.
Gregoire, east from McClellan ave.
Griffin, from Chene, east to Moran.
Griffin, from Wesson ave., west to D., L. & N. R. R.
Griswold, from Detroit river, north to Clifford.
Guilloz, from Pallister ave., north to Whitaker.
Guoin, from 13 Hastings, east to Adair.
Haigh, from Woodward ave., east to Oakland ave.
Hale, from 678 Riopelle, east to Mitchell.
Hamlin ave., from 1624 Woodward ave., east to Hastings.
Hammond ave., from 635 Toledo ave., north beyond city limits.
Hamtramck, east from McClellan ave.
Hancock ave. east, from 960 Woodward ave., east to Mt. Elliott ave.
Hancock ave. west, from 939 Woodward, west to Scotten ave.

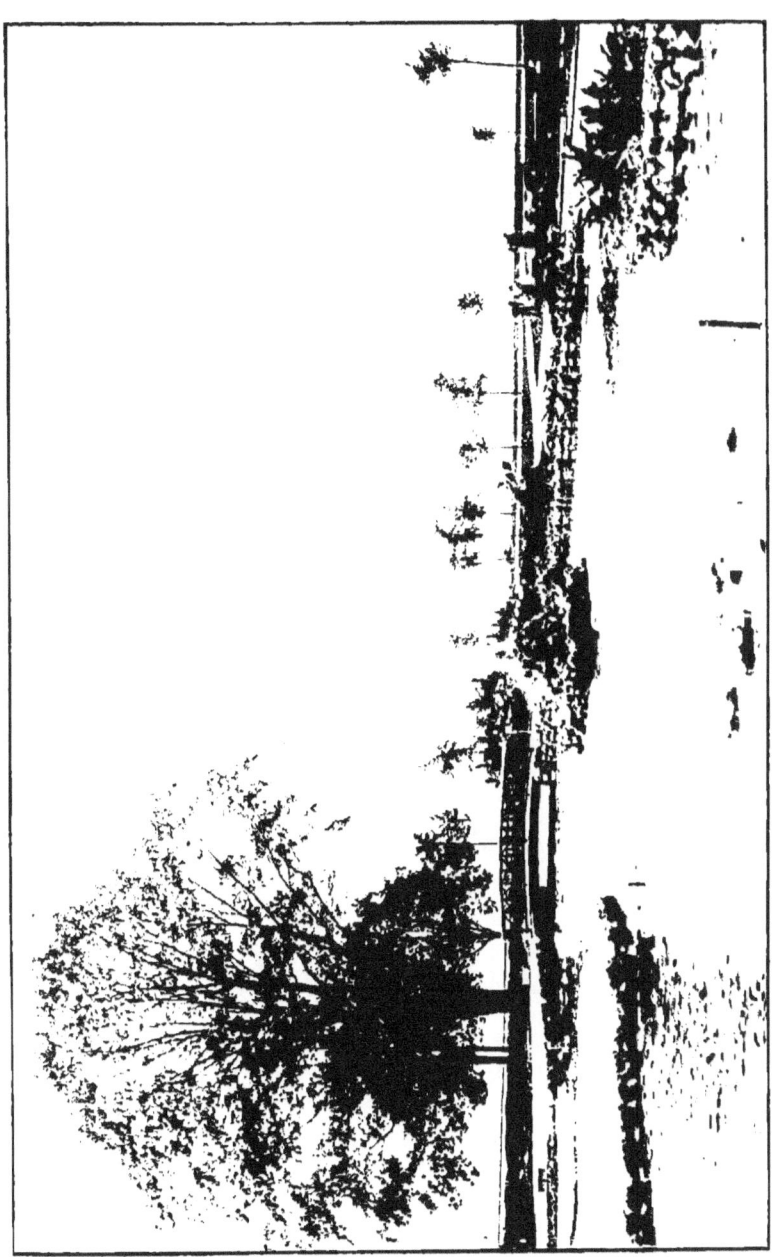

ARTIFICIAL LAKE—BELLE ISLE PARK.

Russell, east to
)m Woodward
l ave.
it, from 1302
east to city
from Twelfth,
n 526 Michigan
ukee ave.
ι Junction ave.,
27 Atwater st.
mits,
ison ave., west
rom Woodward
ird ave.
m Forest ave.,
e.
n 836 Gratiot
ott ave.
1349 Jefferson
r ave.
Woodward ave.,
467 St. Aubin
l ave.
m 1234 Woodelen ave.
from Junction
ell ave.
89 Woodward,
Salle ave., west
:om Livernois,
jouth side Dearbash R. R.
wford, west to
npkin ave., east
n Jefferson ave.,
358 Woodward
ave.
n 347½ Woodhirteenth.

Hoffman, from 708 River, north to Fort.
Holbrook ave., from Woodward ave., northeast to city limits.
Holburn ave., from Ellery, east to Beaufait.
Holcomb ave., from Jefferson ave., north.
Holden ave., from 1195 Woodward ave., west and northwest to city limits.
Hooker ave., from Eighteenth, west to Grand River ave.
Horatio, from La Salle ave., west to Wesson ave.
Horton ave., from 1500 Woodward ave., east to Jos. Campau.
Houghton, from McClellan ave., east.
Howard, from Springwells ave., west.
Howard, from 129 Cass, west to Campbell ave.
Howell, from Michigan ave., north to Vigo.
Hubbard ave., from 1090 Fort west, north to G. T. Ry.
Hudson ave., from 1217 Third ave., west to Vinewood ave.
Humboldt ave., from 819 Michigan ave., north to McGraw ave.
Hunt, from 474 Dubois, east to Mt. Elliott ave.
Hurlburt ave., from Jefferson ave., north to Mack ave.
Huron, from 626 Michigan ave., north to Bagg.
Hussar ave., from Military ave., west to city limits.
Illinois, from Military ave., west to city limits.
Indiana, from 697 Beaubien, east to Russell.
Infantry ave., from Fort, north to L. S. & M. S. Ry.
Ingersoll, from Campbell ave., west to D., L. & N. R. R.
Inglis ave., from Toledo ave., north to Dix.
Iron, from Wight, north to Jefferson ave..

Ironside, from Hammond ave., west to Welch ave.
Irving, from 187 Crawford, west to Eighth.
Irving ave., from Crawford ave., west to city limits.
Ivy Place, from Twenty-third, northeast to Grand River ave.
Jackson, from Scotten ave., west to Campbell ave.
Jameson, east from McClellan ave.
Jay, from 464 Gratiot, east to Elmwood ave.
Jefferson ave., from 31 Second, east to beyond city limits.
Jerome ave., from 249 Piquette ave. east, north to boulevard.
Joe, from 1681 Michigan ave., north to Vigo.
John Edgar, from Junction ave., west to Traffic.
John R., from 236 Woodward ave., northeast to Cross.
Johnson, from rear of 303 Eighteenth, west to Twenty-second.
Jones, from 230 Cass, west to Sixth.
Jos. Campau ave., from Detroit north beyond city limits.
Josephine ave., from Woodward ave., east to Oakland.
Joy, from 545 Cass ave., west to Fifth.
Joy ave., from Crawford ave., west to city limits.
Julia, from Campbell ave., west to D., L. & N. R. R.
Junction ave., from 1483 River, north to Michigan ave.
Kanter ave., from McDougall ave., east to Mt. Elliott ave.
Kercheval, from River road, opp. Exposition grounds, north to L. S. & M. S. Ry.
Kercheval ave., from 490 Mt. Elliott ave., east to city limits.
King ave., from Woodward ave., east to Oakland.
Kinsman, from Scotten ave., west to Clark ave.
Kirby ave. east, from Beaubien, east to city limits.

Kirby ave. west, ward, west to Vine
Knox, from Blai brook road.
Koch ave., from east to Cameron av
Kolb ave., east fr
Labrosse, from 1 to Twelfth.
Ladroute ave., born road.
Lady's Lane, fror Minnie and Swain a Fort.
Lafayette ave., wold, west to Scott
Lafayette Place, ave., west to Scotte
Lafferty, from 60 M. C. R. R.
Lambert ave., fr ave., east to Beaufa
Lambic Place, fro first, west to Twent
Lamson Place, north to Pallister a
Langley ave., fr ave., west to Twent
Lanman, from west to Vinewood.
Lansing ave., fro west, north to Tole
Larned east, fron east to Helen ave.
Larned west, fron west to Fifth.
La Salle ave., fr igan ave, north to c
Lauderdale, from west to Campbell a
Laura, east from
Laurel, from 56 ave., west to Waba
Lawndale ave., n & M. S. Ry., rear tery.
Lawrence ave., f ave., west.
Leavitt ave., fr west to Livernois a

Ledyard ave., from 419 Cass ave., west to Fourth ave.
Lee Place, from Wilson ave., west to city limits.
Legrand, east from Mt. Elliott ave.
Legrand ave., east from McClellan ave.
Leib, from Detroit river, north to Monroe ave.
Leicester Court, from Woodward ave., east to Oakland ave.
Leigh, south from junction of L. S. & M. S. Ry. and Dearborn road.
Leland, from Recreation park, east to Gratiot ave.
Leonard ave., from Fort, north to L. S. & M. S. Ry.
Le Roy Place, from 266 Forest ave. west, north to Hancock ave.
Leuschner, from G. T. Ry., east to Mt. Elliott ave.
Leverett, from 199 Seventh, west to Twelfth.
Leverett Place, rear 250 Twelfth.
Lewerenz ave., from Fort st. west, north.
Lewis, from 205 Cass, west to Fourth.
Lexington ave., from Crawford ave., west to Waterman ave.
Lincoln, west from West End ave.
Lincoln, from D., G. H. & M. Ry., east to St. Aubin ave.
Lincoln ave., from 526 Grand River ave., north to Milwaukee ave.
Linden, from rear of 635 Grand River ave., west to Twenty-sixth.
Linden Court, rear of 36 Linden st.
Linzee ave., from Livernois ave., west beyond city limits.
Livernois ave., from 830 Dix ave., north to city limits.
Locust, from 285 Grand River ave., west to Fifteenth.
Lola, from Wesson ave., west to D., L. & N. Ry.
Lonyo road, west to city limits.
Lorman ave., east from Crane ave.
Lothrop ave., from Woodward ave., west to Twelfth.

Louis ave., east from Crane ave.
Lovett ave., from 1536 Michigan ave., north to Plymouth ave.
Ludden from 918 Gratiot ave., east to Mt. Elliott ave.
Lumpkin ave., north of city limits to Holbrook road.
Lyman Place, from Crystal, east to Orleans.
Lynn, from Oakland ave. east.
Lyon, west from Dearborn road.
Lysander, from 803 Fourth ave., west to Wabash ave.
McArthur Place, from 1512 Twenty-seventh, west to Vinewood ave.
McBrearty Place, from Rivard, east to Russell.
McClellan ave., from Jefferson ave., north to Gratiot ave.
McDougall ave., from 771 Atwater st. east, north to city limits.
McGraw ave., from Sixteenth st., west to Plymouth ave.
McGregor, from Junction ave., east to McKinstry ave.
McKinstry ave., from 1343 River street, north to Toledo ave.
McLean ave., from Woodward ave., east.
McMillan, from Junction ave., west to city limits.
Mack ave., from 962 Gratiot ave., beyond city limits.
Mackie west, from West End ave.
Macomb, from 230 Randolph, east to Elmwood ave.
Madison ave., from 22 Witherell, east to St. Antoine.
Magnolia, from 593 Grand River ave., west to Vinewood ave.
Mansur, from Harper ave., north to Piquette ave.
Maple, from 804 Gratiot ave., east to Concord ave.
Marantette, from 261 Twelfth, west to Fifteenth.
Marcy, from 482 Fourth ave., west to South.
Marietta east, from McClellan ave.
Mark, from 1188 Twelfth, west to Wabash.

STR—STR 62

Market, from High, north to Winder.
Markey ave., from 1855 Michigan ave., north to Pelouse.
Marston Court, from Woodward ave., east to Cameron ave.
Martin ave., from M. C. R. R., north.
* Martin Place, from 698 Woodward ave., east to John R.
Martz ave., from Jos. Campau ave., east to Collins.
Mason east, from McClellan ave.
Maxwell, crosses Mack ave., second east of VanDyke ave.
Maybury Grand ave., from 898 Michigan ave., north to Grand River ave.
Mechanic, from 252 Brush, east to Beaubien.
Mechanic, west from Caroline, west of Exposition Grounds.
Medbury ave., from 1260 Woodward ave., east to city limits.
Meldrum ave., from Wight, north to Gratiot ave.
Merrick ave., from 1012 Cass ave., west to Vinewood ave.
Mersino ave., from Oakland ave., east to Cameron ave.
Messmore, from Boulevard, opposite Eighteenth, north beyond city limits.
Miami ave., from junction of Randolph and Monroe ave., northwest to Witherell.
Michaels, from L. S. & M. S. Ry., west.
Michigan ave., from City Hall, west to city limits.
Middle, from 61 Clifford, southwest to Grand River ave.
Military ave., from 1650 River, north to Toledo ave.
Miller, from 628 Sixth, west to Seventh.
Miller road, from Dearborn road, north to Grand River ave.
Milwaukee ave. east, from 1484 Woodward ave., east to city limits.
Milwaukee ave. west, from 1483 Woodward ave., west to Sullivan ave.
Miner ave., east from Crane ave.
Minnie, from 1160 River road, north to Fort st. west.
Mitchell ave., from 856 Gratiot ave., north to city limits.
Moeller, from Russell, east to D., G. H. & M. Ry.
Mohawk, from Twenty-seventh, west to Vinewood ave.
Monroe ave., from Woodward ave., northeast to Randolph, thence east to Helen ave.
Montcalm east, from 332 Woodward ave., to Russell.
Montcalm west, from 331 Woodward, west to Cass ave.
Montieth, from Twenty-seventh, west to Vinewood ave.
Monterey, from Woodward ave., west.
Montrose ave., from Schmittdiel ave., west to Wilson ave.
Moore Place, from Vinewood ave., west to Thirtieth.
Moran, from 1039 Gratiot ave., north to city limits.
Morrell, from 1447 River, north to Toledo ave.
Morton, from Livernois ave., west.
Morton, from Riopelle, east to D., G. H. & M. Ry.
Mott ave., from Woodward ave., east to Oakland ave.
Mound, north, from Centre Line ave.
Mt. Elliott ave., from Detroit river, north to city limits.
Moyes, from Markey ave., west.
Mulberry, from 793 Twelfth, west to Thirteenth.
Mullett, from 240 St. Antoine, east to Elmwood avenue.
Myrtle, from junction of Grand River and Trumbull aves., west to LaSalle ave.
Nall ave., from 1072 Twenty-seventh, west to LaSalle ave.
Napoleon, from 424 Brush, east to Russell.

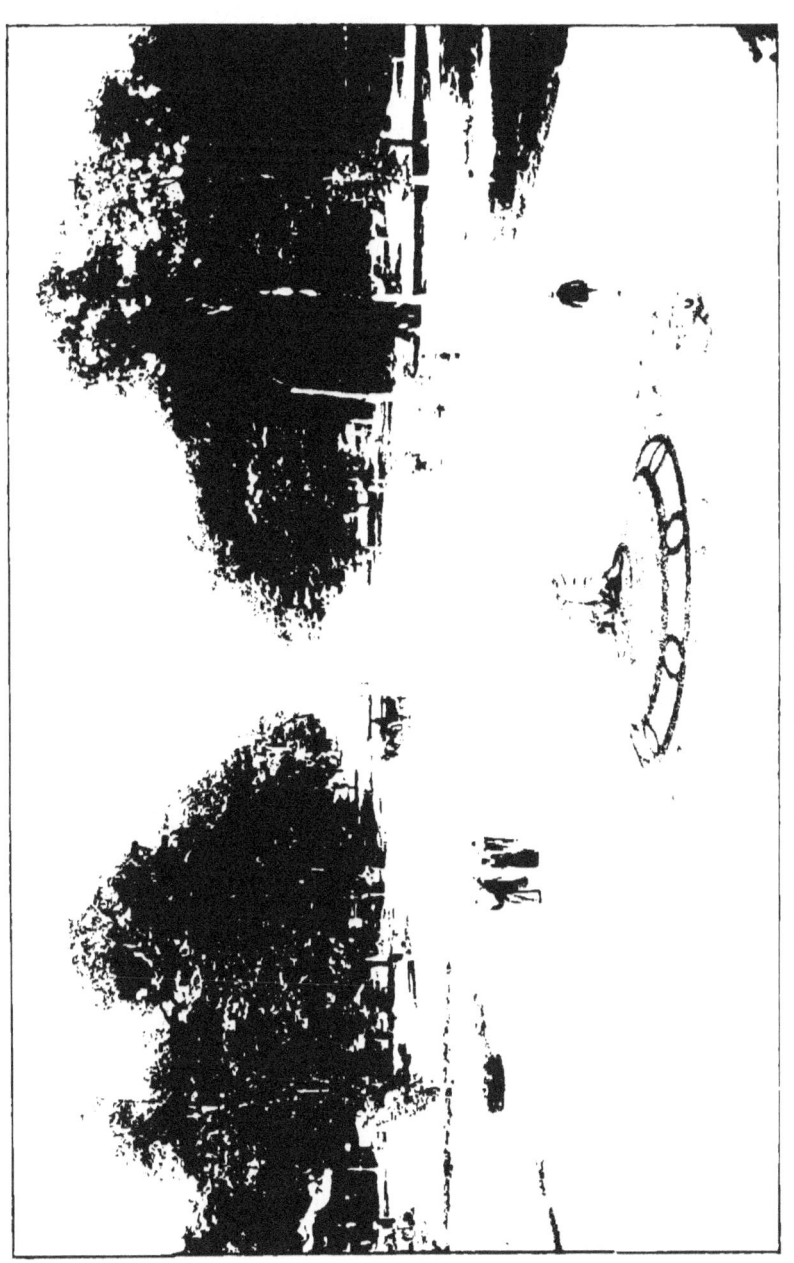

CENTRAL AVENUE—LOOKING EAST—BELLE ISLE PARK.

National ave., from 504 Michigan ave., north to Grand River ave.
Navarre east, from McClellan ave.
Newark, from 205 Fifteenth, west to Twentieth.
Newberry, from Junction avenue, west to Cavalry ave.
Nineteenth, from 792 Fort st. west, north to Newark.
Noble, from 536 Fourth ave., west to Seventh.
Norman ave., from Toledo ave., north to Dix ave.
Norris Lane, from Gratiot ave., and Superior, north and northeast to Mt. Elliott ave.
Norton, from Junction ave., west to D. L. & N. R. R.
Noyes, west from Markey ave.
Oakland ave., from Boulevard, north to city limits.
Oakley, from 1101 Twelfth, west to Wabash ave.
Orchard, from 151 Grand River ave., west to Trumbull ave.
Orleans, from Detroit river, north beyond Pallister ave.
O'Sullivan west, from West End ave.
Otis, from Junction ave., west to D., L. & N. R. R.
Ottawa, from 417 Twelfth, west to Wabash ave.
Owen ave., from Woodward ave., east to Joseph Campau ave.
Pallister ave., from 1664 Woodward ave., east to Jos. Campau.
Palmer ave., from Woodward ave., east to city limits.
Park, from 271 Woodward ave., west and north to Peterboro.
Park Place, from 100 Michigan avenue, north to Clifford.
Parker, from Bellevue ave., east to Concord.
Parker ave., crosses Mack ave. east of VanDyke ave.
Parsons, from 665 Woodward ave., west to Cass ave.
Pelouze, from Livernois ave., west beyond city limits

Pennsylvania ave., north from Jefferson ave.
Perkins, from Livernois ave., west.
Perry, from 373 Grand River ave., west to Humboldt ave.
Peter Cooper ave., from Fort st. west, north to L. S. & M. S. Ry.
Peterboro, from 555 Woodward ave., west to Cass ave.
Peterson ave., north from River road.
Phelps ave., from Holbrook ave., north to city limits.
Phillip, from Columbus ave., west to Minnie.
Pierce, from 631 Riopelle, east to Jos. Campau ave.
Pine, from 315 Grand River ave., west to Seventeenth.
Pingree ave., from Woodward ave., west to Crawford.
Piquette ave. east, from 1366 Woodward ave., east to Mt. Elliott ave.
Piquette ave. west, from 1401 Woodward ave., west to Sullivan ave.
Pitcher, from 585 Cass ave., west to Seventh.
Pleasant ave., from 1201 River road, north to Fort.
Plum, from 321 Second, west to Trumbull ave.
Plumer ave., from Campbell ave., west to Livernois ave.
Plymouth avenue, from Twenty-seventh, northwest to city limits.
Pontiac, east from McClellan ave.
Poplar, from 750 Thirteenth, west to L. S. & M. S. Ry.
Porter, from 187 Second, west to Campbell ave.
Prentiss ave., from 809 Cass ave., west to Fourth ave.
Preston, from 630 McDougall ave., east to Helen ave.
Pulford ave., from 1026 Gratiot ave., south one-half block, thence east to Concord ave.
Putnam ave., from 1021 Woodward ave., west to Tillman ave.

Rademacher, from Hesse, north to Fort west.
Railroad, from 1254 Twelfth, northeast to Holden ave.
Railroad, from LaSalle ave., west to Scotten ave.
Randall, from rear 330 Twenty-second, west to Twenty-fourth.
Randolph, from Detroit river, north to Adams ave.
Rankin, from Rademacher, west.
Ranspach, from Hammond ave., west to Livernois ave.
Rathbone, from West End ave., west.
Raymond ave., from Crawford ave., west.
Rayne, from Hibbard ave., east.
Raynor, from Clinton ave., north to Gratiot ave.
Reed Place, from 1020 Fourth ave., west to Seventh.
Reeder ave., from Junction ave., west to Military ave.
Regular ave., from Cavalry ave., west to Artillery ave.
Reid ave., from Detroit river, north to Fort st. west.
Reutter, from Russell, east to D., G. H. & M. Ry.
Rich, from Twenty-seventh, west to Wesson ave.
Riopelle, from Detroit river, north to city limits.
Rivard, from Detroit river, north to city limits.
River, from 31 Second, west to Delray.
Roby, from 576 Ferry ave., north to Medbury ave.
Rochm, parallel with L. S. & M. S. Ry., from 354 Tillman ave. to Maybury Grand ave.
Rogers, from Junction ave., west to Campbell ave.
Rohns ave., south from Mack ave.
Rollin, from Junction ave., west to D., L. & N. R. R.
Romeyn, from Junction ave., west to Cavalry ave.
Rose, from 335 Sixteenth, west to Twentieth.
Rosedale Court, from Woodward ave., east to Oakland ave.
Ross ave., from Cass ave., west to Crawford.
Rowena, from 630 Woodward ave., east to Riopelle.
Rowland, from 48 Michigan ave., north to Grand River ave.
Rubber, from Markey ave., west.
Russell, from 501 Jefferson ave., north beyond city limits.
Russell road, from Grand River ave., north to Joy road.
St. Antoine, from Atwater st. east, north to Sidney ave.
St. Aubin ave., from 530 Atwater st. east, north beyond city limits.
St. Charles, north from Center Line ave.
St. Clair (Delray), from Kercheval, west to Anderson ave.
St. Clair Place, from rear of 185 Eighteenth, west to Nineteenth.
St. Joseph, from 694 Russell, east to Collins.
St. Paul ave., from 404 Mt. Elliott ave., east to Baldwin ave.
Sargent, from McDougall ave., east to Ellery.
Savoy, from rear of Twenty-first, between Fort st. and Lafayette ave., west to Twenty-fourth.
Schmittdiel ave., from Joy ave., south.
Schneider lane, north from Dix ave.
Schenider Place, from Ellery to Mt. Elliott ave.
Schroder ave., from River, north to Pallister ave.
Schulte ave., from Boulevard, north to Pallister ave.
Scott, from 652 Riopelle, east to Jos. Capmau ave.
Scotten ave., from 1174 Fort st. west, north to city limits.
Scovel place, from Vinewood ave., west to city limits.
Sears ave., east from Hibbard.

Second, from Detroit river, north to 189 Grand River ave.
Second ave., from 190 Grand River ave., north to Boulevard.
Secor Place, from 590 Ferry ave., south to Kirby ave.
Selden ave., from 790 Woodward ave., west to Commonwealth ave.
Seventeenth, from 738 Fort st. west, north to Boulevard.
Seventh, from 324 River, north to Boulevard.
Shady lane, from 381 Twenty-fifth, west to Vinewood ave.
Shelby, from Detroit river, north to Michigan ave.
Sheridan ave., 1479 Jefferson ave., north to city limits.
Sherman, from 298 Hastings, east to Elmwood ave.
Shirlie Place, from Pallister ave., south.
Sibley, from 415 Woodward ave., west to Cass ave.
Sidney ave., from Woodward ave., east to Rivard st.
Sixteenth, from 719 Fort st. west, north to city limits.
Sixth, from 278 River, north to Forest ave.
Smith ave., from 1664 Woodward ave., east to Oakland ave.
South, from 448 Grand River ave., north to Noble.
South, from Artillery ave., west.
Southern ave., from Hammond ave., west to city limits.
Spencer, from 189 Cass, west to Second.
Springwells avenue, from River, north to L. S. & M. S. Ry.
Sproat, from 439 Woodward ave., west to Cass ave.
Spruce, from 405 Fifth, west to Wabash ave.
Spruce, from Fort st. west, south to Wabash R R.
Standish, from 331 Twentieth, west to Foundry.
Stanley ave., from Crawford, west to Twenty-third.

Stanton, from Detroit river, north to 754 Fort st. west.
Stark ave., from Hammond ave., west to Livernois ave.
State, from 163 Woodward ave., west to Cass.
Stimson Place, from 595 Woodward avenue, west to Cass ave.
Stoepel's alley, from Canfield ave., south to Willis ave., between Riopelle and Orleans.
Strong ave., from Mt. Elliott ave., east beyond Belt Line.
Sullivan ave., from 856 Michigan ave., north to city limits.
Sullivan ave. (West Detroit), from Springwells ave., west to Lawndale ave.
Summit ave., from 1398 River, north to Fort.
Superior, from Recreation Park. east to Gratiot ave.
Sutton, from River st., south to Rouge river.
Swain ave., from 1148 River, north to Fort.
Sycamore, from 531 Grand River ave., West to Wabash ave.
Sylvester, from 1118 Gratiot ave., east to Helen ave.
Taylor ave., from Woodward ave., west to Crawford ave.
Tenth, from 436 River, north to Michigan ave.
Thaddeus, from West End ave., west to Dearborn ave.
Theodore, from Day ave., east to Carbon.
Theodore, from 768 John R, east to city limits.
Third, from Detroit river, at M. C. R. R. depot, north to Grand River ave.
Third ave., from 282 Grand River ave., north to Boulevard.
Third ave., from Cass ave., west to Twelfth
Thirteenth, from 456 Howard, north to L. S. & M. S. Ry.
Thirtieth, from 1431 Michigan ave., north to city limits.

Thirty-first, from 1470 Michigan ave., north to city limits.
Thirty-second, from 1508, Michigan ave., north to city limits.
Thirty-third, from 1537 Michigan ave., north to city limits.
Thorburn ave., south from Mack ave., between Baldwin and Van Dyke aves.
Tillman ave., from 956 Michigan ave., north to McGraw ave.
Toledo ave., from 581 Twenty-fifth, west to city limits.
Torrey, from Scotten ave., west to Twenty-eighth.
Townsend ave., from 1514 Jefferson ave., north to city limits.
Traffic, from Detroit river, north to John Edgar.
Trombly ave., from Woodward ave., east to city limits.
Trowbridge, from Woodward ave., east to Oakland ave.
Trumbull ave., from 392 Fort st. west, north to Boulevard.
Tuscola, from 691 Third ave., west to Crawford.
Tuxedo ave., from Woodward ave., west.
Twelfth, from Detroit river, north to city limits.
Twentieth, from 836 Fort st. west, north to Michigan ave.
Twenty-eighth, from 1374 Michigan ave., north to city limits.
Twenty-fifth, from 967 Fort st. west, north to McGraw ave.
Twenty-first, from 866 River, north to Standish.
Twenty-fourth, from 970 River, north to Chope Place.
Twenty-ninth, from G. T. Ry., north to Buchanan.
Twenty-second, from 890 Fort st. west, north to M. C. R. R.
Twenty-seventh, from Michigan ave., north to McGraw ave.
Twenty-sixth, from M. C. R. R. north to McGraw ave.
Twenty-third, from 926 Fort st. west, north to Chope Place.

Union, from 428 Fifth, east to Fourth ave.
Uthes, from Clark ave., west to McKinstry ave.
VanDyke ave., from Jefferson ave., at Toll Gate, north to Center Line ave.
Vernon, from Livernois ave., west beyond city limits.
Vienna, from 1262 Second ave., east to Cass ave.
Vigo, from Wesson ave., west to D. L. & N. R. R.
Vincennes, east from McClellan.
Vinc, from 441 Fourth ave., west to Crawford.
Vinewood ave., from 1072 Fort st. west, north to Grand River ave.
Visger, from 1047 Vinewood ave., west to Thirty-first.
Volunteer ave., from Junction ave., west to Waterman ave.
Vulcan, from D. G. H. & M. Ry., east to St. Aubin ave.
Wabash ave., from 498 Howard, north to city limits.
Walter, from Cass ave., west to Fourth ave.
Warren ave. east, from 970 Woodward ave., east to city limits.
Warren ave. west, from 969 Woodward ave., west to Twenty-fourth.
Washington (West Detroit), from Springwells ave., west to Lawndale ave.
Washington ave., from 68 Michigan ave., north to Park.
Waterloo, from 455 Dequindre, east to city limits.
Waterman ave., from River road, north to Toledo ave.
Watson, from 530 Woodward ave., east to Chene.
Wayne, from Detroit river, north to Michigan ave.
Webster Place, from rear of 133 Eighteenth, west to Twenty-second.
Welch ave., from Toledo ave., north to city limits.
Wellington avenue, from Cameron ave., east to Russell.

CANAL.—BELLE ISLE PARK.

Wesson ave., from 591 Toledo ave., north to city limits.
West (Springwells), from South, south to Noyes' farm.
West End ave. (Delray), from River road, north to Toledo ave.
Westminster ave., from Woodward ave., east to Oakland ave.
Weyher, east from McClellan.
Wheelock ave., from Fort st. west, north to L. S. & M. S. Ry.
Whitaker, from Russell, east to D., G. H. & M. Ry.
White ave. (Delray), north from river.
Whitwood, west from Livernois ave.
Widman Place, from Harper ave., north to Trombly ave.
Wight, from 36 Chene, east to beyond Meldrum ave.
Wilcox, from 206 Woodward ave., east to Randolph.
Wilkins, from 538 Brush, east to Chene.
Wilkins ave., from Woodward ave., west to Crawford ave.
Willett, west from Livernois ave.
Williams ave., from Woodward ave., west to Crawford ave.
Williams ave., from 930 Michigan ave., north to Hudson ave.
Willis ave., east, from 782 Woodward ave., east to Mt. Elliott ave.
Willis ave. west, from 781 Woodward ave., west to Twelfth.
Wilson ave., from Joy ave., south.
Winder, from 392 Woodward ave., east to Orleans.
Wing Place, rear of 211 Eighteenth, west to Nineteenth.
Winslow, from Grand River ave., north to McGraw ave.
Winter, from Dequindre to St. Aubin ave., between Willis and Canfield aves.
Witherell, from 274 Woodward ave., east and north to Montcalm.
Wolff, from Hubbard ave., west to Scotten ave.

Woodbridge east, from 44 Woodward ave., east to Lieb.
Woodbridge west, from 43 Woodward west, west to Second.
Woodland ave., from Woodward ave., east to Oakland ave.
Woodmere ave., from Fort st. west, north to Dix ave.
Woodward ave., from Detroit river, north beyond city limits.
Woodward ave. Terrace, from 678 Woodward ave., east to John R.
Wreford ave., from Eighteenth, west to 1460 Grand River ave.
Wreford Place, from Vinewood ave., west to city limits.
Young, from St. Aubin ave., east, first south of G. T. Ry.
Zender, from Ellery, east to Mt. Elliott ave., between Sylvester and Pulford aves.

Swimming.—(See Baths.)

Telegraph Offices.—Two companies have offices in Detroit. The Western Union, located corner Griswold and Congress streets, and The Postal Telegraph Co., located corner Griswold street and Lafayette ave. The competition of the two companies keep rates lower than they would be if there were only one.

Telephone, Long Distance.— Perhaps the most wonderful thing in this progressive age is the rapid development of the art of telephony. Since the introduction of the telephone, less than twenty years ago, it has been made almost perfect. About eight years ago the first experiments in long distance telephoning were made, and to-day it is possible to talk with people at a distance of 1,000 miles, and the conversation is as intelligible as if the two persons were speaking in the same room.

The six telephone booths are all adjoining, but as the partition walls and doors are made double thicknesses, the booths are absolutely sound-proof. The office is elegantly equipped and thoroughly convenient.

The long distance telephone was opened to the Detroit public on Feb. 18, 1893, Edward D. Trowbridge, manager, and is located at the corner of Griswold and Larned streets. The charge is $2.00 for five minutes.

No charge is made in case the person telephoning is unable to get the man he wants. Appointments to talk are made without charge. The company has a night rate—half rate —from 6 p. m. to 8 a. m.

Eastern states, notably in New England, New York and Pennsylvania, are gridironed with metallic lines connecting with the long distance lines. These lines are adapted for long distance work, and through them can be reached hundreds of points not on the regular long distance lines. The Michigan Bell Company has a first-class metallic circuit to Port Huron and another to Wyandotte, Trenton and Grosse Ile, and more are being built throughout the state.

The American Telephone & Telegraph Company's head office is at 18 Cortlandt street, New York. Its lines extend eastward from New York to Boston, including New Haven, Hartford, Providence, Springfield, Worcester and other important cities. Another line runs from New York to Buffalo via Troy, Syracuse, Rochester, etc. Still another line runs south to Philadelphia, Baltimore and Washington. The main line extends from New York westward to Milwaukee, taking in Reading, Altoona, Pittsburgh, Toledo and Chicago. The Detroit line runs into the main line at Maumee, Ohio, near Toledo.

Telephones.—There are about 4300 in use in Detroit, nearly every business place having one; all drug stores have one, and many other retail stores. No one is allowed by the company to charge outsiders for the use of a 'Phone. Prices for business places range from $72 per year, within half-mile circle, up according to distance; $15 being added for every additional half mile. Residences, $50 per year within half-mile circle, with same rate of increase. The offices are located at the corner of Clifford street and Washington avenue.

Temperature.—The temperature of Detroit, as contrasted with many other cities is very even and healthful. The following data is furnished by the local meterological bureau: Maximum temp. 101°, July 17, 1887. Minimum temp. *-24°, Dec. 22, '72. †Mean annual temp, 48° 1'. †Mean monthly rainfall, 2.73 in. Prevailing direction of wind, s. w. Average daily wind movement, 234 miles.

Average number of rainy days per year, 153.

Theatres.—During the past few years there has been a very decided change for the better in Detroit theatricals, the result is that Detroit, unlike most other large cities, is entirely free from low-class theatres or music halls. Following is a list of Detroit Theatres:

Detroit Opera House, Campus Martius, near City Hall.

German Theatre, corner Russell and Mullett streets.

Lyceum Theatre, Randolph and Champlain streets.

Whitney's Opera House, Griswold street, near Michigan avenue.

Wonderland Theatre in Wonderland Musee, Woodward avenue, near Jefferson avenue.

*Below zero.
†Taken from 20 years' data.

Titles.—The Register of Deeds keeps a record of all titles, deeds and contracts registered with him. His office is located in the City Hall. Heretofore all abstracts have been furnished by the Burton Abstract Agency, but the Union Trust Company recently commenced the enormous undertaking of compiling a new record of all real estate property, going back to the original French owners. This will occupy a large force of clerks about two years.

Tobacco.—Detroit is quite a tobacco centre, there being thousands of Detroiters employed in the factories of this city. The principal ones are Daniel Scotten & Co.
J. J. Bagley & Co.
Banner Tobacco Co.
Globe Tobacco Co.
American Eagle Tobacco Co.

Turners.—There are several large Turner Societies in Detroit, mostly composed of Germans, who hold frequent picnics, with games and other Turner exercises.

Undertakers.—Detroit has her full quota of these necessary people, and one can obtain their services at any time of the day or night. Prices range from a few dollars to several hundred, according to what is desired.

University of Michigan—Is located at Ann Arbor, a beautiful and lively city of 15,000, located on the Michigan Central R. R., about 35 miles west of Detroit. The University is composed of Departments of Medicine, Pharmacy, Chemistry, Agriculture, Law, Literature, and various arts. Students come to the University from all over the world.

Ward Boundaries.—

FIRST WARD.—The first ward shall consist of all that part of the city lying between the center lines of Woodward avenue and Beaubien street, and the said lines extend northerly and southerly to the city limits.

SECOND WARD.—The second ward shall consist of all that part of said city bounded on the east by the center line of Woodward avenue, and on the west by the center line of First street, from the Detroit river to the center line of Grand River avenue, up Grand River avenue to the center line of Second street, and along the center line of Second street, and the said lines extended northerly and southerly to the city limits.

THIRD WARD.—The third ward shall consist of all that part of said city lying between the center lines of Beaubien and Hastings street, and the said lines extended northerly and southerly to the city limits.

FOURTH WARD.—The fourth ward shall consist of all that part of said city lying between the west boundary line of the second ward, above described, and the centre line of Crawford street, from the northerly city limits to the center of Grand River avenue, thence through Grand River avenue to the center line of Fifth street, and down the center line of Fifth street, and said lines extended northerly and southerly to the city limits.

FIFTH WARD.—The fifth ward shall consist of all that part of said city lying between the center lines of Hastings and Russell streets, and the said lines extended northerly and southerly to the city limits.

SIXTH WARD.—The sixth ward shall consist of all that part of said city lying between the west boundary line of the fourth ward, above described, and the center line of Trumbull avenue, and the said lines extended northerly and southerly to the city limits.

SEVENTH WARD.—The seventh

ward shall consist of all that part of said city lying between the center lines of Russell street and Dequindre street, and the said lines extended northerly and southerly to the city limits.

Eighth Ward.—The eighth ward shall consist of all that part of said city lying between the east line of Godfroy farm and the center line of Trumbull avenue, and the said lines extended northerly and southerly to the city limits.

Ninth Ward.—The ninth ward shall consist of all that part of said city lying between the center lines of Dequindre street and Chene street, and the said lines extended northerly and southerly to the city limits.

Tenth Ward.—The tenth ward shall consist of all that part of said city lying between the west line of the Loranger farm and the east line of the Godfroy farm, and the said lines extended northerly and southerly to the city limits.

Eleventh Ward.—The eleventh ward shall consist of all that part of said city lying between the center lines of Chene street and McDougall avenue and the said lines extended northerly and southerly to the city limits.

Twelfth Ward.—The twelfth ward shall consist of all that part of said city lying between the west line of the Loranger farm and the westerly line of the Porter farm, and the said lines extending northerly and southerly to the city limits.

Thirteenth Ward.—The thirteenth ward shall consist of all that part of said city lying between the center line of McDougall avenue and the center line of Mt. Elliott avenue, and the said lines extended northerly and southerly to the city limits.

Fourteenth Ward.—The fourteenth ward shall consist of all that

part of said city lying between the westerly line of the Porter farm and the westerly line of private claim forty-seven, and the said lines extended northerly and southerly to the city limits.

Fifteenth Ward.—The fifteenth ward shall consist of all that part of said city lying east of the center line of Mt. Elliott avenue, and the said line extended northerly and southerly to the city limits; and the parcel of land situate in the Detroit river known as Belle Isle.

Sixteenth Ward.—The sixteenth ward shall consist of all that part of said city lying west of the westerly line of private claim forty-seven, and the said line extended northerly and southerly to the city limits.

Water Commissioners, Board of.—Created in 1853 by act of Legislature at the request of the Common Council, which act was amended in 1873. The Board has the power to provide for the "completion and management of the Detroit Water Works," and for the purpose of "supplying the City of Detroit and without the limits thereof with pure and wholesome water."

There are five members of the Board, chosen one each year by the Common Council upon the nomination of the Mayor, to serve without compensation.

Water Works.—The pumping works are situated in the Water Works Park, four miles east and up the river from the City Hall, and can be reached by Jefferson ave. electric cars. Three engines, with an aggregate daily capacity of 78,000,000 gallons, supply the city, with another in course of construction with a capacity of 25,000,000 gallons.

The average daily quantity pumped in 1892 was 33,634,554 gallons, which was 2,444,612 gallons less than

POLICE STATION—BELLE ISLE PARK

that of 1887. although the population wass about 60,000 more. This was caused by the measures introduced by the Board to restrict waste, which is principally effected by placing meters, over 2,100 being in use January 1, 1893. The expense of operating the works in 1892 was less than $90,000, or about $5,000 less than in 1887. There are now over 431 miles of pipe in the city.

Wayne County Jail—Is a large stone building, with high brick walls around it, and is located corner Clinton avenue and Raynor street. The sheriff's residence adjoins it on the west side.

Whitney's Opera House—Is located on Griswold street, near Michigan avenue, and is a very cosy, well furnished theatre, producing popular plays at popular prices during the season.

Windsor is located on the Canadian side of the Detroit river, opposite the central portion of Detroit. Ferry steamers run every few minutes daily, the year around, between Detroit and Windsor.

Woodmere Cemetery, located in the Township of Springwells, on Fort street west, 4¾ miles from the City Hall, contains 202 acres, about one-third of which has been improved and platted into burial lots; was dedicated and opened to the public July 18th, 1869. Take Fort Wayne & Belle Isle electric cars.

Woodward avenue—Is the principal avenue in Detroit, starting at the river and running straight north through the city and for miles beyond. The avenue from the river to Jefferson avenue is occupied mostly by wholesale houses, from Jefferson avenue to High street, by large retail establishments, and from High street out by magnificent churches and elegant residences, with spacious and well kept grounds.

Wyandotte is a pleasant city of 10,000 population, located on the Detroit river, 10 miles southwest of Detroit. Many Detroiters have suburban residences in Wyandotte, and along the Electric street car line connecting Detroit and Wyandotte. The latter is also reached by the Michigan Central R. R., Lake Shore & Michigan Southern R. R., and in summer by a regular line of steamers. The principal industry at Wyandotte is shipbuilding.

Yachting is a favorite pastime in and about Detroit, the adjoining waters being admirably adapted for the purpose.

A spin across Lake St. Clair to the Flats, on a moonlight night with a fair breeze, is one of the trips that are very often taken, and a trip around Belle Isle and as far as the Grosse Point light cannot be excelled. The cost of running a yacht, where a family or party of friends are accommodated, will compare very favorably with the board bill at any fashionable hotel. There are numerous yachts in and around Detroit, and they present a splendid sight on regatta days, when under way with all sails set. The sails on the ordinary yacht are the mainsail, staysail, jib, jibtopsail, topsail, balloon jib, spinaker and water sail.

There are three yacht clubs in and about Detroit, to-wit.: The Citizens' Yachting, located at the foot of McDougall avenue, the Michigan Yacht Club, located on Belle Isle, and the Detroit Yacht Club. Of these three clubs the C. Y. A., the youngest, has the largest membership, with a splendid club house and largest number of yachts. The duties of a yachtsman, when under way, is to attend to the position assigned him by the captain. An important position is that of steward who attends to refreshments, etc.

Young Men's Christian Association.—The Young Men's Christian Association is the church at work especially in the interests of young men. It endeavors, through its fourfold work, to prevent some from going wrong, to reach and save others that have gone wrong.

The Mental Department has the reading room and library, lectures and evening educational classes.

The Social, its various "Intersocialities," concerts, members' reunions, etc.

The Physical uses as fine a gymnasium as there is in the west, with luxurious shower, sponge and plunge baths attached.

The Spiritual Nature is cared for by the various Bible classes and religious services.

The Association was organized in 1864, incorporated in 1867, and in 1887 dedicated the magnificent building which it now occupies, located corner of Grand River avenue and Griswold street.

S. DOW ELWOOD,　　D. M. FERRY,　　WM. STAGG,　　WM. A. MOORE,
　　President.　　　Vice-President.　　Ass't Sec'y and Treas.　　Attorney

DIRECTORS:

THOMAS W. PALMER,	E. H. FINN,	WM. A. MOORE,
H. KIRKE WHITE,	FRANCIS ADAMS,	JEROME CROUL,
D. M. FERRY,	WM. S. GREEN,	S. DOW ELWOOD.

Wayne County Savings Bank,

DETROIT.

4 Per Cent. Interest Allowed on Deposits.

N. B.—Exclusively a Bank for Savings and Trust Funds.

To the Board of Directors of the Wayne County Savings Bank:

I herewith submit the Forty-Second Semi-Annual Statement of the condition of this Bank, at the close of business January 7, 1893. Very respectfully,

S. DOW ELWOOD, President.

RESOURCES.		LIABILITIES.	
Loans—On Collaterals,	$1,522,043.77	Capital Stock paid in,	$ 150,000.00
"　　On Real Estate,	1,025,914.89	Surplus Fund,	150,000.00
"　　Invested in Municipal Bonds,	2,546,383.18	Reserve Fund,	150,000.00
	$5,094,341.84		$ 450,000.00
Real Estate—Banking House and Lot,	110,000.00	Undivided Profits,	148,874.86
Other Real Estate,	40,148.62	Savings Deposits,	5,741,339.49
Cash on hand,	1,095,783.89	Total,	$6,340,074.35
Total,	$6,340,274.35	**INTEREST.** Due and accrued on Loans and Investments,	$75,000.00

WAYNE COUNTY SAVINGS BANK.

BANKING ROOM AND BUSINESS DEPARTMENT, WAYNE COUNTY SAVINGS BANK.

VIEW OF END OF THE SERIES OF VAULTS, WAYNE COUNTY SAVINGS BANK.

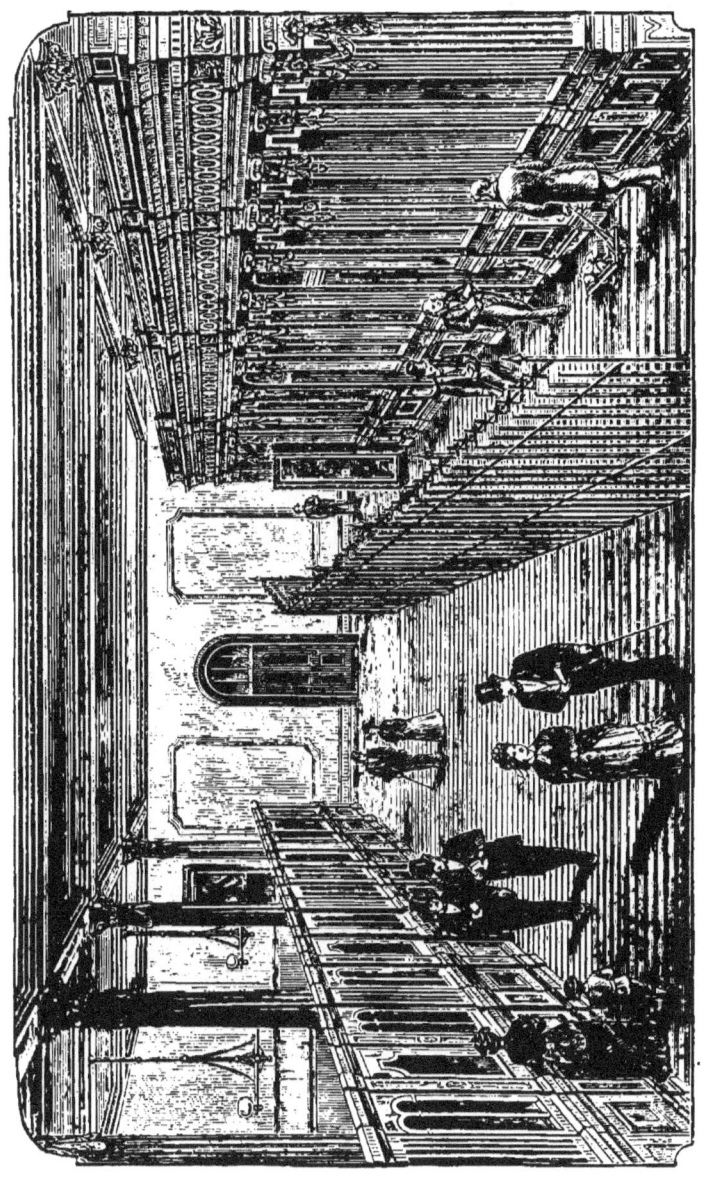

VAULTS AND ENCLOSURE, WAYNE COUNTY SAVINGS BANK.

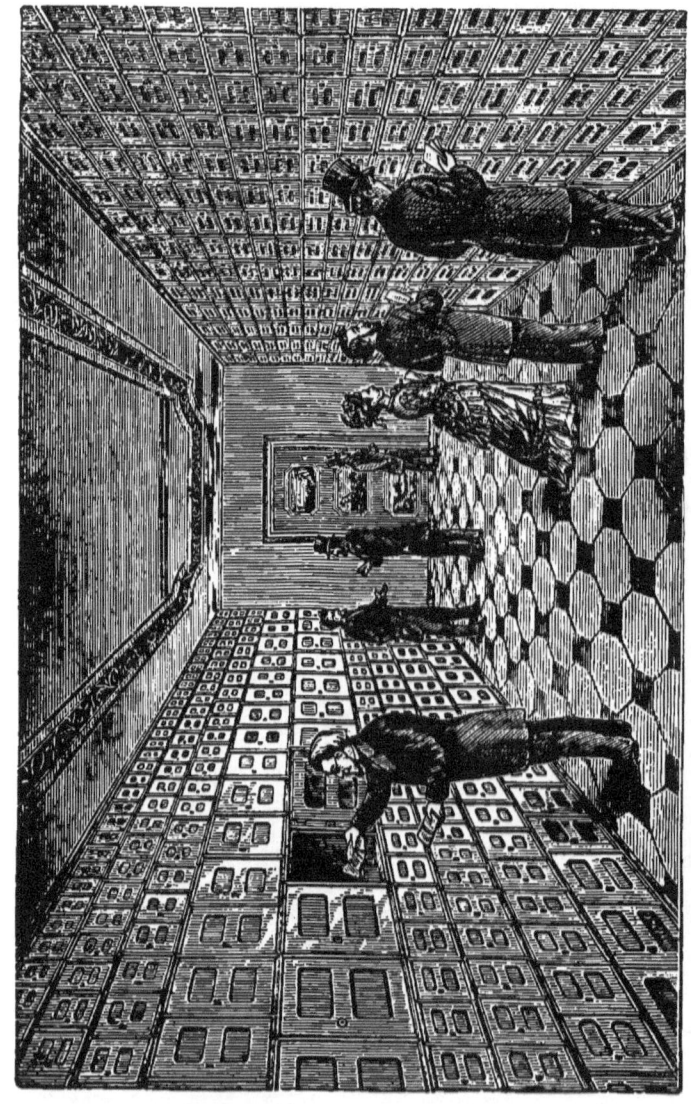

INSIDE OF IRON AND STEEL VAULT, WAYNE COUNTY SAVINGS BANK.

B. GLADEWITZ,

Wholesale and Retail Dealer in

Coal, Wood, Coke and Kindling,

PINE MILL WOOD,

SAWDUST AND SHAVINGS.

MAIN OFFICE:
432 ELMWOOD AVENUE,
TELEPHONE 2254.

YARDS:
432 ELMWOOD AVENUE,
525 GRAND RIVER AVENUE.
33 HUMBOLDT AVENUE.

DETROIT, Michigan.

TELEPHONE 500.

Specialty: WURZBURGER BEER.

912 Beaufait Avenue,   DETROIT, Mich.

OYSTERS
In all Styles.

SANDWICHES
Furnished for Special Occasio

Howard's Cafe,

Home Cooking. Everything First-Class.
Neat and Clean. Finest Cup of Coffee. Ladies! after Shopping
Lunch at our Cafe.

**47
ROWLAN
STREET.**

The National House

MT. CLEMENS, MICH.

A First-Class House where Visitors will find Comfortable Quarters.

Rates from $1.00 Upward.

Situated Near Medea Bath House in the Center of City an Opposite Court House.

Telephone No. 2.

Capital, - - $300,000.00
Surplus and Profits, 60,000.00

THE THIRD ∴ ∴ NATIONAL ∴ BANK
Of DETROIT, MICH.

H. P. CRISTY, President.
   J. L. HUDSON, Vice-President.
      FREDERICK MARVIN, Cashier.
         J. A. DRESSER, Assistant Cashier.

www.ingramcontent.com/pod-product-compliance
Lightning Source LLC
Chambersburg PA
CBHW020131170426
43199CB00010B/724